HAUNTED
WEYMOUTH

HAUNTED
WEYMOUTH

Alex Woodward

First published 2011

The History Press
The Mill, Brimscombe Port
Stroud, Gloucestershire, GL5 2QG
www.thehistorypress.co.uk

British Library Cataloguing in Publication Data.
A catalogue record for this book is available from the British Library.

ISBN 978 0 7524 6046 8
Typesetting and origination by The History Press
Printed in Great Britain

Contents

Acknowledgements

I would like to offer my heartfelt thanks to all the people who helped to make this book possible.

Firstly to the residents, hoteliers, publicans, business owners and various members of staff who live, work or play in the places featured herein. I appreciate the time you took out of your busy lives to talk to me about your experiences, or to point me in the right direction. I've respected the wishes of those who want to remain anonymous and/or have decided to keep the exact location of their experiences unidentified.

I would also like to say how grateful I am to Dave Goulden of Paranormally Active and my son-in-law, Neill Evans, for their research help, and to Ian Brooke for introducing me to the amazing edifice that is the Nothe Fort, and the super bunch of volunteers that work there.

Finally, a huge thank you to my wonderful, long suffering husband Keith, for his constant, unfailing support in whatever I do, and for doing more than his fair share of cooking and housework on account of me being attached to a computer for several months writing this book!

Alex Woodward, conducting a ghost walk at Nothe Fort.

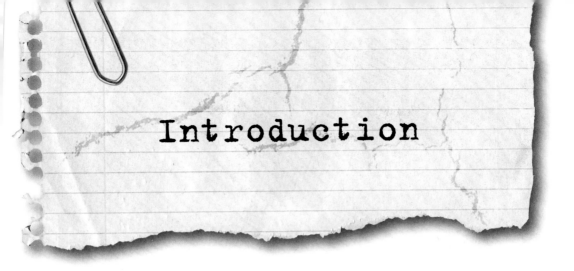

Introduction

To the casual visitor, Weymouth looks every inch a typical traditional seaside town; but it only takes a few gentle scratches to discover, lurking beneath the façade of ice-creams and donkey rides, a history of death, disease, bloodshed and mystery. The town as we know it today once comprised of two independent communities, divided by the natural boundary of the harbour.

Weymouth developed from the twelfth century onwards, on land to the south of the harbour. Meanwhile, at around the same time on the north side, Melcombe started life as a gathering of ramshackle dwellings on a sandy spit of land between the sea and a backwater fed by the River Wey.

While Weymouth seemed to prosper, and boasted a number of fine houses, Melcome became infamous as the port where the Black Death plague entered Britain.

The two towns were never the best of neighbours, and as sea trade grew they regularly fought over ownership of the harbour and the profits it attracted. The bitter, and often violent, rivalry continued until it was brought to an end in 1571 by the intervention of Queen Elizabeth I, who passed an Act which united them into the borough of Weymouth and Melcome Regis.

A rocky peace eventually ensued, and the first wooden bridge spanning the harbour was built in 1594. Less than fifty years later, during the Civil War, the old animosities bubbled back up to the surface, especially as Melcome was under Parliamentarian control and Weymouth was held by the Royalists. A testament to this new hostility can still be seen today, in the form of a cannonball firmly lodged in the wall of a house on the Melcome side in Maiden Street.

The Civil War saw one of the bloodiest periods in Weymouth's history. At one time, a small group of residents formed a plot, known as the Crabchurch Conspiracy, to oust Cromwell's forces from the town and bring it back into Royalist hands. The battle lasted for many days, resulting in a huge loss of life and the conspirators' plans being thwarted.

After the monarchy had been restored, Weymouth and Melcombe were reputed to have such a high level of alcoholism that local taxes were raised significantly, in an attempt to bring drinking under control. In addition, the area was a haven for smugglers, who had the

The Civil War cannonball is still lodged in the upper wall of a house on the corner of Maiden Street and St Edmund Street. It is believed to have been fired from the Weymouth side of the harbour, towards the town's old adversary Melcome Regis.

pick of coves and deserted hidden beaches to bring their booty ashore for sale to a thirsty and plentiful populace.

A significant change to the fortunes of Weymouth occurred in 1789, when King George III made his first visit to the town. The King became so attracted to Weymouth, partaking in daily dips in the waters from the golden sands of the beach, that he holidayed in the town every year and purchased Gloucester Lodge, on the Melcome seafront, from his brother. Where the King went, the high society of the day followed, and the town rapidly grew to cater for the ladies and gentleman coming to take to the waters. Thus Weymouth and Melcombe Regis was firmly established as one of England's first holiday resorts. Land was reclaimed from the sea on both sides of the town, to satisfy the need for further expansion.

Prosperity followed in the wake of the booming holiday trade, and the revenue for local hotels and the port was further enhanced when a steam-packet service began a regular crossing to the Channel Islands and the railway came to the town.

Sadly, the Second World War saw a rapid decline in holiday trade and, before long, the beach sported coils of barbed wire and anti-invasion devices. Dog fights took place over Portland, and soon streets were filled with GIs stationed around the town in preparation for the D-Day landings. Between 6 June 1944 and 7 May 1945, nearly 500,000 troops and 150,000 vehicles left for French beaches via Weymouth.

After the war, Weymouth settled back into doing what it does best; providing everything needed for a great family holiday. There are still donkeys and deckchairs on the beach, but these have been joined by a variety of twenty-first-century amusements, and as the town readies itself for the 2012 Olympic sailing events, everywhere is getting a brush-up and a re-vamp.

The stories of ghostly happenings and reports of mysterious events in this book are a combination of local legends, well-documented case histories, and actual firsthand accounts gathered during my research for the Weymouth ghost walks, and later for this book. A number of them were also experienced or witnessed by myself personally. In as many cases as possible, I have sought to include as much background or historical information relating to the event as I have been able to discover.

I lived for a number of years in a house where a great many odd and rather spooky things happened, so I have a belief in the paranormal based on experiences I cannot reasonably or rationally explain, and while I subscribe to there being 'more things in heaven and earth', I am not attempting in this book to prove the existence of ghosts, monsters or other phenomenon. I have only intended to put forth the facts, as told to me in good faith or as I have uncovered through research, and then leave it for you to deliberate.

So whether you are a sceptic, a believer, or not too sure, one thing is certain…at the end of this book you will never see Weymouth in the same light again!

One

Around the Town

Nothe Fort

The Nothe promontory, overlooking the harbour entrance, has featured some form of building or fort, linked with defending the town and surrounding area from coastal attack, since at least the fifteenth century.

The present fort dates back to mid-Victorian times, when fear about the strength of the French Navy prompted the building of defences all along the south coast. Although the threat of invasion by our cross-Channel neighbours had passed by at the time it was built in 1872, the Nothe Fort saw action during the Second World War and troops were stationed there until 1956. In 1961, the Ministry of Defence sold the fort to Weymouth Council and it succumbed to vandalism and disrepair. Weymouth Civic Society, along with Manpower and a host of interested individuals, rescued the fort from total dereliction in the late 1980s, and now maintain it as a museum and tourist attraction.

Since times still in living memory, the Nothe Fort has had a reputation for strange ghostly happenings, and it now attracts a steady stream of paranormal investigators and events. English Heritage voted it one of the UK's top ten haunted sites.

Nothe Fort.

Side view of Nothe Fort as it stands on the headland overlooking Weymouth Bay.

The bridge over the approach to Nothe Fort.

Would you dare to enter Nothe Fort in the dead of night?

One of Nothe Fort's underground passageways.
This one is said to be home to the Whistling Gunner.

The Whistling Gunner

This is the oldest and most talked about of the fort's ghost population. Legend has it that in the late Victorian times, a young gunner was helping to lift one of the heavy cannons up to the gun deck by means of a rope hoist. The rope broke and the cannon fell, killing the gunner outright.

As the unfortunate young soldier was apparently an expert and avid whistler in life, he remained so in death and for decades his eerie whistling in the fort's subterranean passageways has been heard by those stationed there, as well as by present-day volunteers and visitors. Nowadays, a recording of whistling is played during daylight opening hours in the underground passageways, but on a couple of occasions when visitors have remarked about the whistling, members of staff have later found the tape player to be switched off. Similarly,

faint tuneful whistling has been heard on many occasions by both staff and investigators long after the fort doors have been closed for the night.

Madam

No-one is sure to which of the fort's eras this lady belongs; all anyone knows is that she is a lady who will make her feelings strongly known to those who do not afford her the respect she believes she deserves, or if there is something happening in the fort that she is unhappy with. Several years ago, groups of new volunteers made their way into the canteen area through the parade-ground door, carefully closing it behind them. The group had only walked a few paces into the room when the door sprung wide open. One of them turned back to shut the door, only for it to spring open again moments later. This happened several times and eventually one of the group members fetched a maintenance man. Instead of setting about fixing the door catch as they expected, the fellow instructed them to go back out onto parade ground and then return indoors, this time saying 'Good morning madam' as they passed over the threshold.

The volunteers were a little sceptical, thinking it was perhaps some sort of 'newbie' prank, but nevertheless they did as they were told. They were, however, not so sceptical when the door remained firmly shut after the last person had closed it behind her.

'Madam' also plays havoc with the CCT video cameras by switching them off if she is displeased, and only when staff have apologised to her will things return to normal.

The Black Shadow

In 1983, a young teenage boy found his way into the abandoned fort and decided to have a look round. He'd heard a lot about the place, as his father had served there during the war. The derelict fort, with its overgrown ramparts and waterlogged passageways, had become a secret playground for local youngsters, and this boy was no exception. One afternoon in late autumn, after playing in the fort, he decided to make his way home as it was turning dusk. Before leaving, however, he felt a compelling need to turn round. In doing so he got the shock of his life. Standing at the edge of the parade ground was a tall, indistinct man-shaped black shadow. He watched, transfixed, as the shadow moved across the ground, and he was horrified when the thing came to a halt and turned to look at him before carrying on with its journey, eventually disappearing into one of the empty old store rooms. When asked how – if this shadow had no form or face – did he know it was looking at him, the boy replied that he just felt very strongly that it had, like a sort of psychic connection. Far from being put off from ever going to the fort again, he returned many times, but never again did he see the walking black shadow.

Shell Store

Situated off one of the underground tunnels, this former shell store consists of nothing more than four bare whitewashed walls, a ceiling and a stone floor. A least likely looking candidate for a haunted location you would be hard pressed to find, yet this room has played host to many strange and unexplained happenings. On 12 June 2010, as part of the fort's 150th anniversary celebrations, this author undertook to perform a series of 'ghost talks' in the room, recounting local ghost stories as well as those from the fort itself.

Nothe Fort parade ground. Here it is set up for an open-air production of The Tempest, but it is also the site of a very scary real-life encounter in the 1980s.

Having forgotten to wear a watch, I kept my mobile phone on a nearby table. As each talk was to last no more than forty minutes, it was important to keep an eye on the time. Unfortunately, within a matter of fifteen minutes my phone battery was dead, completely drained of the full charge it had received the previous evening. Over the course of the day, the phones of three other visitors suffered the same fate, along with several cameras.

It is common too for some people to suddenly get a bad headache and/or feel ill in this room. On that day, I suffered a constant headache from almost the moment I entered the room until I left for a break midway through, only to have it return shortly after resuming the talks. Two other people that day were not so lucky. One gentleman felt so ill he had to be escorted to the surface. He complained of a blinding headache, nausea and dizziness, which only started just after he'd entered the room. Another person (a radio presenter recording the event for hospital radio) felt similarly ill, but not as intensely, and he was able to carry on recording.

In one particular corner of the room, visitors also complained of being touched on the back; one young woman suffered the unsettling attention of a ghost cheekily blowing in her ear! The fort is a dog-friendly attraction and on two separate occasions that day, dogs became very agitated in that corner and would not settle until their owners moved to another spot. There was also a boy of around two years old, who, while waiting with his parents for the talk to begin, kept turning and waving to an unseen something in the same corner. When asked who he was waving to, he replied 'Man' and giggled.

Following the success of the anniversary celebration ghost talks, it was decided to do a similar event on two nights over the Halloween period. Again, the room did not disappoint. Those attending complained of back pain and a heavy feeling in the legs, with one woman reporting that the pain and heaviness was very severe. All recovered, thankfully, when back on the surface in the refreshment area. Several people pointed out that while the fronts of their bodies were quite warm, their backs felt absolutely icy cold, as though they were standing in front of an open freezer.

The strangest phenomenon, however, must be 'the sway'. I'd felt it myself earlier in the evening while placing a lantern in the room. When standing, it seemed as if the room was leaning very slightly and I felt the need to 'go with the room', so it became quite hard to keep balance. On each occasion that visitors were brought into the room during the event, many of those present felt a similar effect (to

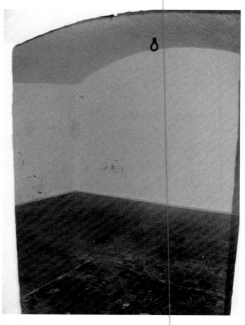

Shell Store B9. Countless strange happenings have occurred in this innocent-looking room.

a lesser or greater degree). During one episode, a fort volunteer was standing outside the doorway and he felt the room swaying too; he said it felt like a tremendous energy emanating from the space. In all his years as a volunteer he'd never experienced anything like it.

It's worth pointing out that at no time, either during the June talks or the Halloween events, was anyone told what previous visitors had experienced. The people who complained of back pain did so privately to me and independently of each other.

Nothe Gardens

The tranquil headland boasts spectacular scenery, but this place has a darker side too. In recent years, there have been regular reports from those walking the area in the half-light of early morning, of seeing what seem to be two men duelling with swords. The men are described as wearing clothes similar to those worn in the Regency period. They do not interact with anyone, but simply engage in swordplay before fading from view.

The gardens were once the site of the town gibbet and saw the execution of several of the Civil War Crabchurch Conspirators (see Chapelhay section) and from my own experiences, this area does seem to have a high incidence of strange happenings.

On 3 July 2009, I was recounting the final part of the conspiracy story, very near to the site where the gibbet is reputed to have stood. Without warning, one of the group shouted out in alarm that her mobile phone was vibrating. Indeed, it was, but she was startled because it was actually switched off! She removed it from her bag and, to the amazement of the others in the group,

it continued to vibrate for several seconds. On further examination, I can confirm that it was indeed switched off.

It is also in that area that some of those attending the ghost walks experience strong feelings of déjà vu. One gentleman made it very clear at the start of the walk that he was only attending to accompany his wife, who was interested in the subject. He was not a believer and thought ghosts and the paranormal 'a load of old hooey'. However, while in the Nothe Gardens during my recounting of the conspiracy story, I could see he was becoming quite agitated. After I had finished this particular section, I asked him if anything was wrong as he still seemed upset. He replied, quite forcibly, that he didn't know me, had never been to Weymouth before and had certainly never heard of the Crabchurch Conspiracy, yet as I was recounting the story on the headland, he knew every word I was about to say and he could see very clearly in his mind's eye what had happened there all those hundreds of years before. He explained it was like a film being shown in his head, but with the soundtrack (my voice) delayed by a few moments.

Of the others who have reported feelings of déjà vu in this area, none shared his vivid 'film' experience; most claim to simply have the feeling that they know what will be said next, as if they have heard the story before. Others claim to have suddenly felt very sad or angry as they have approached that particular spot, with one lady actually breaking down in tears. It's worth noting that those who experienced feeling emotionally volatile were affected on arrival at the spot, before they heard the story. It's also notable that, while the story of the Crabchurch Conspiracy is in the public domain, it remains very much a local story and one which you would have to have at least some awareness of in order to discover all the relevant details. With the exception of only one person, all the people who reported experiencing *déjà vu* or unfounded feelings have been visitors from other parts of the UK.

Although my public ghost walks do not feature interaction with live actors or the employment of special effects, one year I decided to 'spice up' our Halloween walks. I'd heard a story from Edwardian times about a gentleman, named only as 'John', who fell in love with a local lady employed as a laundress in the Nothe Fort. The tale goes that they became engaged and then one day, he waited on the bridge overlooking the path leading to the fort entrance in order to surprise his betrothed as she left work for the day. Unfortunately, it was John who was surprised – by the sight of his love walking out arm-in-arm with one of the soldiers. Driven mad by this betrayal, John later lay in wait for the soldier and killed him.

The plan was for someone to dress up in black Edwardian clothing and to wait on top of the bridge while I, at the entrance of the Nothe Fort, recounted stories of the various ghosts inside. At the end, I would tell the tale of 'Black John' and, at a given moment, I would point in horror at the bridge; the crowd would turn to see a ghostly apparition rising up, waving a large axe at those gathered below.

It was meant as a little bit of seasonal fun, but the actor playing 'Black John' was not amused when, while waiting on the bridge for us to arrive at the fort entrance, he heard footsteps approaching along the seaward path leading up to the bridge. Not wanting to alarm anyone as he was dressed in black and carrying an axe, albeit a fake

Nothe Gardens. This is reputedly the site of the town gibbet during the Civil War, where several members of the Crabchurch Conspiracy were hanged.

one, the actor hid in nearby bushes. The footsteps, however, did not pass by as he expected; instead they stopped beside the bushes. For several agonising moments, the actor waited for the footsteps to continue, but when they did not he decided to risk peeking out from the bush, fully expecting to find someone standing there. To his amazement, there was no-one there and he appeared to be alone on the bridge.

I am assured by this person that there is no way he imagined the footsteps or misheard the sound. The night was silent; there was no breeze to rattle surrounding trees, and as he had made his way through the gardens and up to the bridge, he did not see anyone else in the vicinity other than myself and the ghost-walk group, standing at the old gibbet site.

An interesting addendum to this story is that, while the actor was experiencing these phantom footsteps, one of the ghost walk group stopped my recounting at the gibbet site to say that they had just seen a black shadow walking across the headland towards the bridge. I silently cursed the actor for using the seaward path and not the more hidden landside path to get to the bridge as instructed. After the event, he told me about the footsteps and I rebuked him for using the wrong path and being seen. The actor insisted that he had used the landside path to the bridge and, quite rightly, pointed out that if he had walked the seaward one, due to the layout of the gardens, it would have been impossible for him to have accessed this path without cutting across the group.

Needless to say, this actor was reluctant to reprise his role the following year. Thankfully, a replacement was found, but he was not told of his predecessors experiences. 'John' 2010 arrived somewhat early for duty and decided to sit and wait on a bench situated on the landward path. While sitting there, he had the uneasy feeling of being watched, but put this down to the darkness and the proximity of the trees creating an eerie atmosphere. Despite this rationalisation, the feeling persisted, so he decided to go up onto the bridge. However, while waiting there he too heard footsteps approaching from the seaward path; but instead of hiding, he turned to see a man coming across the bridge. As it was a very dark night, he could not see exactly what the man was wearing, just that is seemed to be some sort of dark, longish jacket with trousers and no hat. Similarly, the man's facial features were also non-descript – other than his 'full set' beard and moustache. As the unknown man passed by, 'John' wished him goodnight, to which the man looked and nodded in his direction before walking on towards the landside path. John's attention was then momentarily distracted by the sound of our group arriving at the gibbet site, and when he turned back, the man had disappeared. John had a clear view of the landside half of the bridge and path, and as it had been only a mere second or two that he had looked away, the man should have still been visible.

Friends Burial Ground

Situated along Barrack Road, this disused burial ground has now been turned into a peace park. As the name suggests, the burial ground was originally the property of the Society of Friends, better known as the Quakers. In addition to burials of those in the Quaker faith, plots were also generously extended to those of no fixed religion, and several unknown bodies of shipwreck victims are alleged to have been buried here. When the society felt unable to maintain

The Society of Friends burial ground.

Grave stones recovered during the recent burial-ground renovations.

the ground, it was gifted to Weymouth and Portland Borough Council and the headstones were removed. These were piled up in one corner and left to disappear under a mound of brambles and weeds.

From the time of the headstones' removal, there have been reports of muted voices, taps and touches, and this has been borne out by both this author and those attending my ghost walks. Out of respect to those who are resting there, I always ask for a moment's silence when we enter the ground, and it is during this time that several people have heard snatches of childish giggling. The ground is walled all the way around, save for a narrow entrance. Apart from a few trees, the whole inside area is visible. When this giggling was heard, I can categorically confirm that no children were present either inside or out. With regards to taps and touches, I am usually facing the people present as I recount the history of the burial ground, and I can also confirm that no human person could be responsible for making these taps and touches.

One of the strangest phenomenon here is photographic. Numerous orbs of varying sizes have been caught on camera on nearly every ghost walk, and it is usual for people to discover that, while photographs taken before and after visiting the burial ground are absolutely fine, those taken inside the boundary are very often blurred or out of focus. Two particular instances do warrant special mention. The first was a photograph taken of a ten-year-old boy attending the walk. The resulting shot showed the perfectly clear image of the boy set against an out-of-focus background, almost giving the impression he had been superimposed. If that wasn't enough, the outline image of the boy was very bright, as if he was omitting an aura. The second photograph that stands out as being particularly odd was during a walk on which we were accompanied by Steven Griffiths, presenter of Living TV's programme *Living With The Dead*. He was not on the walk through any official capacity, just as a normal visitor. On entering the burial ground he asked me if there had ever been reports of a ghost dog, as he felt a dog's presence strongly in one corner. I said that to my knowledge and experience there were no such reports. Within a few moments, two young men also attending the walk showed me a photo they had taken on one of their mobile phones.

One of many orbs photographed in the burial ground during our ghost walks.

In the picture there was the distinct sight of two small, glowing, parallel red dots, a few inches apart from each other; they seemed to be hovering just above the level of the long grass. The site of the dots was the same corner where Steven Griffiths had felt the presence of a dog. On inspecting the area quite thoroughly, we could find no explanation; there was nothing physical to reflect a camera flash, nor was there anything red and/or shiny hidden in the grass.

The Seagull Café

This traditional takeaway chippie with a small restaurant in Trinity Street, is famous amongst locals and visitors alike for serving tasty fish and chips. Late one night, not too long after the present owner moved in, he was convinced he'd left the fryers switched on and came downstairs to check. In order to get though to the frying area, one has to

The Seagull Fish & Chip shop, haunted by a cheeky old man with a love of salt.

first walk though the restaurant. On opening the door into this area, the owner was startled to see the figure of an old man sitting at table No. 2. The old man seemed aware of the owner too as he looked round, smiled and promptly faded into thin air. The only trace of him was the salt he'd sprinkled all over table No. 2.

Although the old man is very rarely seen, he makes his presence felt on an almost weekly basis by leaving a good dusting of salt on table No. 2. He seems to be a benign but mischievous old fellow as, in addition to the salt sprinkling, he also likes to pat or blow into the ear of the owner's wife when she stands doing the ironing or some other household task in the upstairs apartment. Once he even whispered a cheeky 'boo' behind her.

The Old Rooms

The present Old Rooms public house is part of a much older building dating back to Elizabethan times, when it was first a private house and then served as Weymouth's Assembly Rooms until 1785.

For many years there have been sightings of a ghostly woman in the ladies' toilet. No-one can say for certain who she is, as there are no reports of any female deaths or other traumatic events involving a female in that part of the property. By all accounts, she initially appears quite solid, and although witnesses cannot say exactly what she is wearing, they do have the impression that it is not anything that could be described as 'period'. The lady is either already in the washbasin area when someone first goes in there, and then promptly fades away, or else she appears momentarily smiling behind you when you are washing your hands.

*The original Assembly Rooms (Old Rooms)
entrance (c. 1760).*

*The Old Rooms public house,
formerly the Assembly Rooms.*

While the vast majority of reports come from the experiences of adult females, a young girl of six years old, who had gone to the toilet on her own, is reported to have told her mother about a 'really nice' lady in there, who was dressed in posh clothes and had smiled at her. The mother was seated where she had a clear view of the door to the toilets and was sure that no woman of this, or any, description had gone in or out the toilets while her daughter was in there.

The experience leaves witnesses bemused rather than frightened, as all agree that the lady is neither threatening nor unpleasant in any way.

Hope Square

Up until near the end of the eighteenth century, the old harbour had a larger inlet on the Weymouth side than is obvious today, which was known as Ope Cove. The inlet ran inwards as far as the area where the Red Lion public house stands today. Following major reclamation of land in the nineteenth century, much of Ope Cove was filled in to form what is now known as Cove Street and Hope Square.

In between the Red Lion and the Crows Nest restaurant, there is a narrow alleyway leading down to the harbour. On the red brick walls of the Red Lion, in the alleyway, are numerous carvings of initials, some reputed to date back to the Second World War, when the pub was a favourite among American servicemen stationed in the town prior to their D-Day embarkation to the Normandy beaches.

There have been many reports of a pungent, unexplained smell emanating along the alleyway, which is described as being akin to the aroma of strong tobacco, similar to American cigarettes. The smell comes and goes very abruptly.

Hope Square. This area was once an inlet, or 'ope', off the main harbour, where 250 Irish Mercenarys met their deaths during the Civil War.

It is worth noting at this point that the reports of the tobacco smell do go back very many years, to long before the present ban on smoking in public buildings, so it cannot easily be attributed to smokers standing outside either the Red Lion or the Crow's Nest. The smell also comes and goes very suddenly; one witness, who encountered the smell while walking along the alley, stated, 'It was like walking into and out of a cloud of freshly exhaled pipe tobacco smoke, but there wasn't any actual cloud.'

Another witness, who was sitting outside the pub very close to the entrance to the alley, actually remarked to her friend, 'what on earth is someone smoking down that alley?' as the smell was so powerful. The friend agreed and leaned back in her seat to have a look, only to discover that there was actually no-one in the alleyway.

Is the smell a 'scenting' from a young GI, far away from home and on the verge of a major battle he felt he may not return from? Did he stand in the alleyway, carving his initials on the pub wall for posterity, while perhaps enjoying a calming cigarette? Or is the smell associated with a much earlier war?

The area is very popular with holidaymakers as there are small tea shops, restaurants, pubs and the award-winning Brewers Quay attractions lining the square. But how many of those sampling the delights of a Dorset cream tea, or a refreshing beer, realise that they are sitting in an area with an exceptionally grisly past, harking back to the Civil War and one of the bloodiest nights of the Crabchurch Conspiracy campaign?

After losing ground in High Street, the Royalists at last seemed to be making headway, as 250 Irish mercenaries, fighting on the side of the conspirators, fought their way from the Nothe down into Weymouth. However, their luck ran out when they met with Cromwell's troops coming the other way, and a short but bloody fight took place. The Irishmen were beaten back, fired on and driven over the quayside into the freezing February waters below. All 250 perished in the cold waters of Ope Cove and no record was made of what happened to their bodies. Some say they were never recovered from the cove or given a Christian burial, their corpses left floating until they eventually sank to rot on the sea bed. Some also believe that their remains were not even removed when the infilling took place.

I have it on good authority that musket fire has a pungent smell similar to that of strong tobacco. Is the scent therefore another, much older, soldier's way of reminding the living of the area's past?

Brewers Quay

Beer has been brewed in the vicinity of the present-day Hope Square since at least 1252. The last company to operate a brewery there was Devenish, which ceased production in 1985. The site was sold to developers, who reopened the main building in 1990 as Brewers Quay, a complex consisting of an array of specialist shops, The Timewalk (a walk-through exhibition featuring scenes from the town's past), a brewery exhibition, Weymouth Museum, a pub and a restaurant.

While the developers maintained the brewing theme, it seems that the spirits of those that once worked in the brewing industry there were maintained too, as the building is renowned for unexplained happenings and ghostly presences that have made themselves known to both staff and visitors alike.

Brewers Quay. These former brewery buildings were transformed into a shopping village, where the long-dead former employees still roam the corridors and offices.

The Village Store

Specialising in delicacies, real ales and baked products, the 'store' is housed in the oldest part of the building, and staff, when opening up in the morning, often find jars and other items neatly stacked on the floor. Packets regularly fall off shelves of their own accord and occasionally, much to the alarm of visitors, some goods will actually fly halfway across the room before dropping to the ground.

One member of staff seems to regularly attract the attention of a cheeky spirit there in the form of having her apron strings tugged or pulled completely loose.

Staff also report seeing what appears to be a customer at the counter when they look through from a rear preparation area or have been engaged in another part of the shop floor, but when they arrive to serve, they find no-one there and the store empty. This 'mystery shopper' has also been known to queue up with other customers. One visitor, when asked by the store assistant what she would like, pointed out that it was the gentleman next to her who was first; she was very disconcerted to find that he had vanished!

Global Crafts

This area has seen perhaps the most instances of ghostly activity from at least 1992 until the present day. During the early 1990s, the rear of the store was stocked with traditional wooden toys, children's books

The Village Store, one of the oldest and most paranormally active parts of Brewers Quay.

and teddy bears, and when staff opened up they would quite frequently find one of these books lying open on the floor in that area and a doll placed alongside. Curiously, they noted that it was always the same book and was always open at the page, which bore a picture of a dog.

Whoever was haunting the shop at that time also had an opinion on where stock should be placed, as when the teddy bears were moved to shelves on the opposite side of the shop, one particular (and quite large) bear would be removed and placed back where it had been displayed originally. The spectral 'remerchandising' carried on almost daily, until the bears were moved to a different shop in another part of the building.

As with the Village Store, female assistants in Global Crafts also attract ghostly personal attention. One long-serving member of staff often had the side of her hair and face stroked, while another receives friendly taps on her shoulder or tugs on apron strings. Both of these staff members are not frightened by the experience, having become accustomed to it over the years. However, there have been occasions when female customers receive and tap or pat on the back instead, and are quite unsettled to turn and find no-one there!

When working alone in the shop, usually at the beginning or end of the day before customers arrive, staff will also hear the metal coat hangers rattle in the clothing section, vague whispering, and the sounds of things being picked up and placed back on shelves. This activity usually stops when they acknowledge the presence by saying hello or politely asking for it to stop.

A medium visited the building and claimed to have made contact with a male spirit called Jack, who was in life a cooper employed at the former brewery. Jack admitted to being the one who tinkers with stock and disturbs female assistants. Unfortunately, it was not made clear whether the spirit haunts just this particular shop only or the whole building.

The medium also stated that it was definitely not Jack who was responsible for the open book and the moving of teddy bears, but felt that is was a 'young spirit', whom she could not fully connect with. Considering it was a child's book and toys that were being affected, this could be an easy conclusion to make, but the image of a child has been glimpsed in various parts of the building, along with the sounds of childish giggling. The child is reputed to be that of a girl, between the ages of five and eight. She is dressed in a crinoline-type white dress and has long blonde hair.

Brewers Quay staff have christened her 'Matilda', and she is reputed to be the daughter of a former brewery manager who became lost in the building one time when her father brought her into work. Local legend suggests that poor Matilda met her end by drowning in a vat of ale, as her body was only discovered when the brew has been drawn for bottling. No-one knows if she fell in by herself or was disposed of in there by the perpetrator of some terrible deed against her. Legend, rather gruesomely, has it that the manner of Matilda's demise was kept secret and the brew sold as normal to an unsuspecting public, who declared it one of the finest tasting ales ever produced.

More recently, the rear of the shop houses a display of wind chimes and decorative garden stakes. Jack, Matilda, or whoever, has now turned their attention to these, with one very large chime being singled out. Members of staff report this chime sounding when no-one is close by, and even though it is near to an open entrance, they doubt it is draft which is responsible, as all the other much lighter and smaller chimes remain silent. Staff and visitors have also witnessed the central thick wooden striker suddenly start to swing back and forth, gathering pace until the chimes are activated; again, all the other chimes remain silent.

Similarly, should staff physically stop the chime, the hanging price tag and label attached to one of the decorative garden stakes starts to flap and twist as though caught in a strong breeze. It's quite a startling sight to those not used to it, as there are at least two dozen other identical stakes displayed and their tags and labels remain perfectly still.

The Timewalk

This is an all-weather visitor attraction depicting scenes from Weymouth's past, where it's not uncommon for these scenes to come to life – and this is not courtesy of the animatronics cat, Mrs Paws, who acts as your guide in each section. Several members of staff over the years have reported strong feelings of being watched in the reception area. Popular rumour is that the unseen eyes belong to Gabrielle, the brewery engine-house worker, who died when his long muffler became entangled in the beam-engine machinery that once stood in what is now the reception area.

Throughout the years the attraction has been operating, visitors have spotted the figure of a shabbily dressed woman standing near to the cart collecting the plague dead. She is looking down, so her face cannot be fully seen. The woman stands very still, giving the appearance of being one of the mannequins in the scene, but then turns her head to one side and vanishes. Needless to say, those visitors who received slightly more than they have paid for make the rest of their way through the Timewalk at a brisk pace!

Ladies' Toilets

Built into a vaulted area on the ground floor are the ladies' public toilets, and they've long held a reputation for having an eerie atmosphere. Visitors, including myself and Brewers Quay staff, have experienced the feeling of someone standing behind them as they wash their hands, and fully expect to see a person reflected in the mirror when they look up from the basin. Bearing this in mind, it was with little surprise that on 29 October 2010, one of the administration staff opened an email enquiring if any strange activity had ever been reported in the ladies' facilities. The writer was a gentleman enquiring on behalf of his wife, who had experienced the most unsettling feeling of being poked in the back while she was sitting on the toilet! In addition to this rather rude paranormal encounter, she also experienced the usual feeling of someone behind her while she washed her hands.

Staff Only Areas

Out of public sight in the building's upper floors, lies a veritable warren of corridors leading to offices, staff rest rooms and stockrooms. One consistent sighting in the vicinity of the administration office is that of a tall, slim woman dressed in what seems to be an Edwardian high-neck blouse and long straight skirt. She is seen to be carrying a tea tray, complete with cups, along the corridor and fades when approached. Occupants of this office have often noticed a shadow passing by the open door, as if someone has walked past, but when they look or call out, no-one is there.

The stockroom, known as 'Hope', houses not only a selection of goods for each store, but also a playful ghost which will move steps, pull and tug at clothing and stack items as in the Village Store. On a few occasions, female staff members have been alarmed by an unseen person blowing in their ear.

There are plans to extensively refurbish the building in 2011, and to incorporate both hotel rooms and apartments. It will be a massive undertaking, with some features disappearing forever. Employees have noticed that whenever there is any talk of the forthcoming works, paranormal activity normally follows almost immediately, with either something being thrown off a shelf or an unexplained sharp noise sounding nearby. It certainly does give the impression that the resident spirits of Brewers Quay are not happy at the prospect of future upheaval, and one wonders what will happen when the work commences, and afterwards.

Chapelhay Steps

A popular route of stone steps leads from the Town Bridge up to the area known as Chapelhay, and gentlemen using this route to come down into Weymouth should take extra care!

A total of three men, walking down into the town in 1983, 1997 and as recently as 2008, report that at a certain point about halfway down they felt themselves suddenly pushed rather roughly in the middle of their backs by an unseen hand, causing them to almost miss their footing and fall the rest of the way to the bottom. Fortunately, all were able to regain their balance and thus avoided suffering any major physical injury.

Prior to the push, they were not aware of anyone behind them, and after recovering they did not see anyone when they turned to give the pusher a piece of their mind.

It may be just coincidence that all three lost their footing at a similar point and each subconsciously imagined there was a push, but other men have reported an 'odd' feeling on the steps, with one stating, 'Them steps are not right.' If the pushes and odd feeling are of a paranormal nature, there may be a couple of reasons.

The present route beside Holy Trinity Church has moved from its original setting. A decision was made, in 1870, to improve access to Chapelhay and eventually, some years later, plans were put forward for this to be carried out. In 1884, some houses just to the west of the church were demolished. We could presume that the ghostly pusher is a former resident of one of those houses, still angry that his or her home was pulled down to make way for the new route.

However, this would not explain why it is only men who seem to be affected. According to local legend, there was a 'quack' doctor who practised in rooms next to the old steps. One theory says it is a ghost of a woman from the notorious backstreets of nearby West Plains, who had visited the 'quack' and died as a result of a small operation he'd performed on her. She is said to haunt the steps, looking to extract revenge on the doctor and violently pushing anyone who resembles him.

14 Rodwell Avenue

Along this busy thoroughfare lies the former home of George Joseph Smith, the infamous 'Brides in the Bath' murderer. He came to Weymouth on 22 August 1910 with his fiancé, Bessie Mundy.

The same unremarkable-looking terraced house was also once home to another newly married couple, who, after moving there in the early 1930s, began to experience a downturn in their relationship. Without any known reason, both began to feel increasingly depressed and tired; they later described feeling as though life was being sucked out of them. Soon the tiredness led to irritability and, although they were previously very happy together, they found themselves arguing, often over trivial matters.

Divorce in those days was generally not an option, so they continued to live together, albeit unhappily, until one night, while brushing her hair in front of a mirror before getting into bed, the wife saw the ghostly face of a dark-haired woman standing behind her. The wife let out a scream, which alerted her husband to her side. That night she was so upset by the experience, she lay closer to her husband than she had done in many months.

In the following days, there were no sightings of unknown faces in the mirror and the event was put down to the stress of the current domestic situation, but later

Chapelhay Steps. If you are a man, you had better watch your step as you go down!

that month the ghostly face struck again, only this time it was seen looking through from the outside of a rear window. More sightings happened in the following weeks until, unable to stand both the ghostly face and the arguments, and against all that was at that time socially acceptable, the wife packed her bags and left the house.

Her husband very quickly came after her, and after talking things through decided to move out of the house and set up home elsewhere. Within a few weeks, they moved into a small cottage in Wyke Regis and found that the depression and feelings of exhaustion rapidly lifted and their relationship returned to its previous close and loving state.

They lived in the cottage for the rest of their married lives and raised a family there. In the early 1980s, she revealed to her soon-to-be married granddaughter that she felt the house in Rodwell Road was poisoned in some way and that it was the house that was responsible for the black moods, and consequently the near break-up, of her marriage.

When asked by her granddaughter if this had been the reason for the move to the cottage, the older woman went on to talk about the reccurring face of a woman reflecting off mirrors, windows and newly washed glassware. It was this regular, chilling apparition that had led to her leaving. The granddaughter told me that her grandmother was thankful to whoever the poor woman was in life, as she considers that the ghost actually helped to save her marriage by forcing her, and her husband, to leave the toxic atmosphere.

In researching the background of this house to see if there was any historical reason why the house might have had such a depressing effect on the inhabitants, I discovered that it was the one-time home of a notorious serial killer. Was the dark-haired woman, therefore, the spirit of poor Bessie Mundy, and did she indeed try to save a young couple from heartbreak by haunting them until they left? Although Bessie was not killed in that house, she did know great sadness there.

George Smith, using the assumed name of Henry Williams, married Bessie on 26 August at Weymouth Registry Office. The new Mrs Williams could not know that she was her husband's sixth wife, and that hers was the first of three of his marriages that would end with murder. Smith, who had been in trouble since the age of nine, was a charmer who married for money, and when he had drained his wives dry financially, he moved on to seek another.

Bessie had an inheritance of £2,500, but try as he might Smith could not get his hands on the money. While living at Rodwell Road, he persuaded Bessie to give him £150, and when she did he left her, accusing Bessie of infecting him with a venereal disease. The broken-hearted Bessie remained in the Weymouth house and eighteen months later, in 1912, while walking through Weston-Super-Mare, she caught sight of her husband. Smith turned on the charm and Bessie allowed him back into her life — what she had remaining of it!

Less than a week after their seaside reunion they moved to Herne Bay, where they rented comfortable rooms, and as they had no access to a private bathroom, Smith visited the local ironmongers to purchase a tin bath. Ever the devoted husband, Smith had taken Bessie along to the doctor in Weymouth and Herne, stating that she was suffering from fits, although Bessie complained only of headaches. Medication was prescribed, but not long after the visit to the doctor, Bessie was found dead in her bath and the doctor pronounced 'drowning due to epilepsy' as the cause of her death.

George went on to marry Alice Smith in 1913, and Margaret Lofty in 1914. Both of these brides also suffered from 'fits', and, according to George, he found himself widowed after his wives drowned in their baths during a presumed epileptic episode.

It was only by chance that an eagle-eyed reader of the *News of The World* noticed that the death of Margaret Lofty was very similar to that of Alice Smith the previous year and informed the police of his suspicions.

Scotland Yard investigated and arrested Smith, as it seemed perhaps a fellow could not be so unlucky as to lose three wives to the same end, especially as all three had substantial insurance policies paid out to Smith on their deaths, in addition to him inheriting Bessie's £2,500!

The Home Office pathologist Sir Bernard Spilsbury was brought in to discover the murder method. In turn, he examined the exhumed bodies of Margaret, Alice and Bessie. He observed that no blunt instrument or force had been used to kill or stun the women prior to drowning, and from details given in the reports of the doctors who attended the deaths, neither did it seem likely that they had fought against being pushed under the water. After tests, poison was also ruled out.

Sir Bernard believed that while these women had indeed drowned, it was not caused by them slipping under the water during a fit. Quite the contrary in fact, Sir Bernard discovered that the first stage of an epileptic fit consists of a stiffening and extension of the entire body. Considering Margaret Lloyd's height (5ft 7in) and the length of the tub (5ft), he ascertained that during a fit the upper part of her body would have initially been pushed up the sloping head of the tub, far above the level of the water. The second stage consists of violent spasms of the limbs, which are drawn up to the body and then flung outward. Therefore, no-one of her size could possibly get underwater, even when her muscles were relaxed in the third stage – the tub was simply too small. Although Bessie and Alice were smaller in stature, the stiffening and extending of their bodies during a fit would still have pushed them up above the water rather than under it.

Sir Bernard was baffled. He was now certain that Smith had murdered all three, but he had to prove it. Firstly, he ordered the tub in which Margret Lloyd had died to be sent to London. Next, he measured the deceased women and hired several experienced female divers of the same size and build as the victims. Aided by Inspector Neil, Sir Bernard experimented with how possible it was to get them underwater in a way that would not leave the inevitable signs of struggle. Eventually, Neil leaned over one of the divers who was relaxing for a few moments in the bath, and without warning, pulled both of her feet sharply upwards. Her head glided underwater before she knew what happened. Sir Bernhard saw that the woman was no longer moving and quickly pulled her out. It took him and a doctor over half an hour to revive her.

Sir Bernhard and Inspector Neil had at last discovered Smith's *modus operandi*. Each unsuspecting victim would have lain quite relaxed in her bath, maybe watching as her loving husband leaned towards her as if to deliver a kiss. Instead, he would have seized her by the feet and suddenly pulled them up towards him, sliding the upper part of her body underwater without fuss. The sudden flood of water into her nose and throat would have caused sudden loss of consciousness; drowning would have quickly followed.

George Joseph Smith was tried and found guilty, on 1 July 1915, of killing all three women. The death penalty imposed upon him was carried out in Maidstone Prison shortly afterwards.

The Boot Inn

Standing at the end of Weymouth's original High Street (now renamed High West Street), The Boot has the reputation of being Weymouth's oldest, and also its most haunted, inn. The building dates back to the seventeenth century and is believed to be home to several ghosts and a poltergeist.

In November 1973, the then new licensees, Mr and Mrs Ratcliffe, were woken on two successive nights by the sound of heavy footsteps clumping around in the bar. Mr Ratcliffe went to investigate, but saw nobody, though the heavy tramping on the floorboards could clearly be heard. The previous licensee had warned them that they might hear the faint sound of sea shanties being sung when the bar is seemingly empty.

In July 1977, The Boot Inn's poltergeist mystery came to light once again. Mr and Mrs Smith, who had taken over the running of the pub, reported experiencing a whole host of uncanny happenings, including locks being tampered with, doors opening and closing at will, wall decorations being moved, and even furniture being rearranged. During a recent paranormal investigation by a local internet TV company, unexplained knockings, footsteps and voices were recorded, along with a wall light flickering on and off by itself.

The barmaid once saw a ghostly resident as she changed a barrel in the cellar. Shortly after the incident, Mr Smith went to the same spot and suddenly felt an intense cold come over him. He looked over his shoulder and for a split second saw the apparition of a seaman, wearing heavy sea boots.

Today, the cellar is described as having a brooding and malevolent atmosphere, and staff dislike going down there alone. A medium, who paid a visit to the inn while on holiday in Weymouth, later confided to me that she felt as if the spirit in the cellar belonged to a revenue man who had been in the pay of the smugglers and landlord of The Boot. The revenue man had become a little too demanding in regards to the cost of him turning a blind eye, and so a meeting was arranged in the cellar to discuss the new 'terms'. On his arrival, several men jumped him and his throat was slit. His body was never found; it was assumed by his superiors that he had abandoned his position and left the area.

In addition to long-dead seamen and customs officers, one of the ghosts is thought to be a lady of easy virtue, who sits in the corner waiting for her lover who was drowned at sea.

The hauntings are not confined to the inside of the building; the yard is allegedly haunted by the figure of a coachman who was last seen about ten years ago.

Smugglers Tunnel

Newton's Cove is a small, secluded area on the old Weymouth-side of the town. It was once the perfect spot for landing smuggled goods away from the eyes of the Revenue Men and, if local myth is to be believed, there was an underground tunnel built to transport the booty from the cove (or in some versions it is a cave underneath the nearby Nothe Fort) and the cellar of The Boot Inn at Rodwell. The myth also maintains that several houses built above the route had access to the tunnel too.

No evidence of a tunnel opening or cave exists today, as the tiny beach and

The Boot Inn, reputedly Weymouth's oldest and most haunted inn.

rocky inlet that formed the cove has been obliterated by the concrete of a recent promenade-style development. However, while researching information for the ghost walks, I heard that prior to the development, sightings of shadowy figures had regularly been seen moving about on the beach at night. At first it was assumed they were local youths, but then those watching observed the figures walking out into the sea and fading into thin air. The figures were once spotted during the Second World War and a policeman was summoned amid fears that Germans were about to invade; however, the figures vanished and, although a thorough search of the area was made, nothing and no-one was found.

There may be some truth to the existence of a secret tunnel, as during my research I had the good fortune to speak to a lady, now in her late eighties, who remembered visiting her uncle's house with her father as a young child. The house stood in West Plains, which is now called North Quay. The lady recalled that on one of their visits, her uncle and father took up a large stone slab from in front of the fireplace and proceeded to disappear down into a hole. Curious as to where they had gone, she followed them down a very narrow set of steps and found herself in what looked like a small room with walls that were rough to touch. Leading off this room was a sort of corridor, and she could see the glow of a lamp in the distance and the shadow of her uncle and father. She again went to follow, but the noise of her footsteps made the two men turn round.

The girl was scolded by her father and taken back above ground. She was told to never tell anyone about the cellar or the tunnel, and that if she did she would be in for a 'gert hiding'.

An interesting addition to this story recently came to my attention by a former occupant of one of the properties adjacent to the Municipal Office car park. She remembers, on occasions, hearing noises coming from under the ground floor. She said it sounded as if something was being dragged, and from time to time there was also a faint but distinctive thumping. Thinking there may be vermin under the floorboards, she called in a pest-control company, but no evidence of any infestation was found.

If the tunnel stories are to be believed, then the present-day Municipal Offices and car park are built over its purported site, on land that was provided by the compulsory purchase, and subsequent demolition, of the houses in West Plains. During the eighteenth and nineteenth century, the area had the dubious reputation of being inhabited by petty criminals, prostitutes, smugglers and those up to no good. It was a myriad of small streets and courts, but the only physical remains today are the back walls at the rear of the car park.

Love Lane

This pretty little street, lined with tiny cottages and small quaint houses, is reached by way of a steep set of steps off the old Weymouth High Street, and has its origins in the early seventeenth century. Many residents from nearby Chapelhay use the street as a cut through on their way into town, and one such young man did exactly that in the summer of 1976.

It was around 7 p.m. when Peter Dean turned into Love Lane on his way to meet friends in the Belvedere pub, which lay close to the bottom of the steps. On his way towards the steps, he saw a young woman approaching from the opposite direction. Peter was quite taken with how she looked and gave her a smile as they passed; he was very pleased to see his smile returned. A few paces later he turned to speak to her – maybe she'd like to go to the pub with him. Unfortunately, when he turned round she had gone. As it was too quick for her to have reached the end of the lane, he assumed that she had gone into one of the cottages or houses and thought no more about it.

A few weeks later, Peter was again walking down Love Lane at around 7 p.m. when he spied the same young woman walking towards him. He made the decision to speak to her this time and as she drew close, Peter stopped and smiled. Sadly, this time his smile was not returned and she quickly passed. He immediately turned to say 'hello' and, to his amazement, she had disappeared. Peter is now in his fifties but has never forgotten the pretty young woman. He is quite sure that there is no way she could have slipped into any of the houses the second time they'd met, as she had been almost right beside him. He describes her as having very dark hair, cut into a short bob, and, although she seemed normal in every way, he did think that her clothes were a bit old fashioned; in a time when most girls were wearing long maxi-skirts and flowing tops, she was wearing a skirt above the knee and a sleeveless fitted top, similar to the fashion of the previous decade.

Quite who this young woman was has never been discovered, and even though Peter continued to use Love Lane for several years, until he married and moved to a

Love Lane. Will you encounter a lovely lady there too?

different area of Weymouth, he did not see her again. Was she a ghost or did the young man experience a time slip? One thing is for sure; the young man never forgot the lovely lady of Love Lane.

Chapelhay

Chapelhay is an area of Weymouth that has seen more than its fair share of bloodshed, through two terrible wars 300 years apart. On the night of 17 November in 1940, tons of bombs were dropped in an air raid on the town. A huge parachute mine exploded over Chapelhay with devastating effect, destroying many houses and the local school. Twelve people were killed and over forty seriously injured. The raid changed the area forever, as the ruined buildings were cleared and replaced by the flats we

can see today towering on the hill behind the Municipal Building.

But it is believed to be the events of a much earlier war that are felt in the modern-day Chapelhay. During the Civil War, Weymouth and Melcombe Regis were governed by Colonel William Sydenham, and a large Parliamentarian contingent was stationed in both towns. This was not to the liking of local resident Fabian Hodder who, along with his wife and several others, hatched a plot to rid the towns of Cromwell's men and bring them back once more into Royalist hands. Their plan became known as the Crabchurch Conspiracy.

The Battle of Weymouth began at midnight on 9 February 1645, and an army of conspirators, Royalist sympathisers and soldiers from the Royalist garrison on Portland, launched surprise attacks on the Parliamentarian forts at the Nothe and Chapelhay, which led to the capture of both of these crucial strongholds. However, Major Francis Sydenham (the governor's brother) escaped capture and began to rally Roundhead support.

Leading from the front, Sydenham spearheaded a counter-attack upon the Cavaliers, who had captured the powerful Chapel Fort of St Nicholas. A fierce and bloody fight ensued, but the Chapel Fort remained in Royalist hands and the Roundhead's inspirational and much admired leader, Francis Sydenham, was mortally wounded.

William Sydenham, along with Thomas, the youngest Sydenham sibling, vowed to avenge their brother's death through a carefully considered strategy. Helped along by mistakes and misjudgements of an over confident Royalist contingent, this aim was fulfilled some eighteen days later, but not after much bloodshed and considerable loss of life. After a very brief time back in the hands of the Royalists, the towns were once more under the control of Cromwell. The Crabchurch Conspirators and their sympathisers were hounded down and brought to justice with an appointment at the Nothe gibbet.

Late one February evening in 1983, Sarah Miller was walking to her home in Franchise Street after a night out with friends. Apart from feeling chilly, which was normal for that time of year, Sarah was quite happy and relaxed. Little did she know something was to happen which would send that chill right through to her bones. Just before arriving at the flats where she lived, she suddenly heard the sound of heavy footsteps and the laboured breathing of a group of people running up behind her. Sarah turned to see what was going on and to step out of their way, but instead of people, all Sarah saw was the empty street.

In February the following year, a male resident of Franchise Street was awoken at 3.30 a.m. by the sound of shouting and general disturbance. Whatever the season, the man always slept with this window open a little, and so was used to hearing the usual noises of the night and of people making their way home from one or other of the nearby public houses. Rather annoyed to be roused from his sleep, he went over to the window fully intending to shout a piece of his mind to those causing the rumpus outside. He was shocked, however, to find no-one there. Even more curious was that the noise continued and, although the man could not hear individual words, the voices had a definite angry and urgent edge to them.

Thinking that the sounds were most likely being carried on the breeze from Weymouth town centre, he returned to bed only to be awoken twice more. The last time he also heard the sound of a beating drum.

Later the following week, the resident remarked to a friend about his disturbed night when there was 'something going on' down in the town. The friend then told him that it was nothing to do with noises being carried up on the breeze and everything to do with noises being carried by time. The friend lived in Chapelhay Flats as a child, and had been woken several times over a number of years by angry shouting and what seemed to be drumbeats. A couple of times he was frightened to hear what sounded like gunfire. The friend is convinced that the noises are echoes from the Civil War battle that took place in Chapelhay, but his parents always claimed they were nothing more than his own imagination, or remnants of a nightmare.

It is said that traumatic events, or states of intense emotion, become imprinted in the fabric of the area, and due to a reason, or reasons, as yet not known, the imprint – in this case a sound recording – is replayed. There is no doubt that the historic battle in this area was indeed savage and bloody, with a high death toll. However, there is very little that remains of what could be considered the fabric of Chapelhay during 1645. Could the events of that night be imprinted in the actual ground?

Lost Treasure

Chapelhay actually takes its name from the Chapel of St Nicholas, which once stood there. History tells that pilgrims, travelling from the port of Weymouth to the shrine of St James at Compostela in Spain, would make the uphill trek to the chapel to pray for safe passage. The pilgrims, of course, would also leave an offering, usually gold or some other precious item. Legend has it that when Cromwell's forces took Weymouth, the priests hastily buried the casket containing the offerings, in order to save it from falling into Parliamentarian hands. The priests hoped to return to dig up the casket once Cromwell had been defeated and when a King sat once more on the throne of England. Sadly, the chapel, converted into a fort by General Sydenham, was so badly damaged that the priests never returned.

If you believe the tale to be true, then somewhere in Chapelhay lies a treasure trove just waiting to be discovered!

East Street

Situated on the Melcombe Regis side of the town, this street has the dubious title of 'Weymouth's most haunted street', boasting a total of no less than six haunted buildings.

Unknown House
In 1861, a case of poltergeist activity took place at Weymouth in a house on East Street. Numerous people witnessed the nightly activity of crockery rattling and knocking on walls. One man fired a pistol at the spot where he heard the knocking

East Street, possibly the most haunted street in town!

and was amazed when the ghost caught the bullet and threw it back at him. The poltergeist activity only stopped when a hysterical girl left the house.

The Globe Hotel
Although the present owners have never personally experienced any paranormal activity, one of their cleaners repeatedly saw a young girl of around seven years old in the bar area, dressed in Victorian-style clothes. There is never any interaction, and the child is always the same; she appears towards the back wall at the side of the bar, runs on a diagonal path through the bar room and fades near to the door.

It was discovered that what is now the bar room was once the accommodation for the landlord and his family, so it could follow that this child is simply running through what was once her living room.

Given all this information, it seems the ghost of the Globe Hotel may be classed as a 'recording'. It is a well-known theory among paranormal investigators that there are apparitions who show no knowledge of their surroundings and often appear to follow different room layouts from the existing ones. They repeat exactly the same actions whenever they are seen, just as if they had been caught on some sort of spectral video tape – hence the term 'recording'.

Templemans Mill
In the late 1980s, a young man rented the top floor of a newly converted apartment block. For several months he enjoyed peaceful, undisturbed sleep, until one night he was awakened by a low rumbling sound coming from the ceiling. The rumbling stopped almost as soon as he had opened his eyes, so he assumed it was a dream and settled back to sleep.

A few weeks later, he was awoken again by the same low rumbling, which seemed to increase and decrease in volume for several minutes before silence reigned. As his bedroom lay directly beneath the flat roof of the block, he reasoned that the most likely explanation was something rolling about in the wind up and down on the roof.

Unconcerned, he continued to hear the rolling/rumbling on an occasional basis and always put it down to the same reason. However, within a few months of the first occurrence, he was being woken by the nocturnal rumblings on an almost nightly basis. One night the rumblings continued for much longer than normal and sleep became impossible. He convinced himself that it was not a 'something' that was rolling about up there, but a 'someone'; perhaps skateboarders had gained access and were using the flat roof as an unofficial skate park.

He got out of bed, dressed, and made his way to the roof-access door. He threw it open, ready to challenge whoever he found. To his amazement, he was greeted by silence and no-one in sight. He walked around the roof and soon came to the conclusion that he was entirely alone and, not only that, he found nothing at all, no debris or other object, that could account for rumblings.

Unfortunately for the young man, the nightly activity continued with increased intensity and he started to suffer from lack of undisturbed sleep. Unable to stand it any further, and with the uneasy knowledge that there was no reasonable explanation for the noises, he quit his tenancy and moved.

Research has uncovered that this building was once a flour mill, and originally had two further upper floors which suffered serious fire damage in 1917. The two floors

Templemans Mill.

were finally removed in 1937 to form a flat roof above what would become the young man's apartment. Could the unexplained noises be attributed to echoes of the building's past incarnation? The lost floors have now been rebuilt to make a spectacular penthouse apartment, and the whole building has been refurbished.

The Turks Head

Now a private house subdivided into flats, this building was once The Turks Head coaching inn.

In the 1970s, a young family bought the property, which was then being run as a guest house. At first it was only the husband who lived there, as there was a large amount of renovating and redecorating to be done. The rest of the family would take up residence once the work was completed.

One night, as he settled down to bed, he heard the sound of footsteps coming up the stairs. Thinking someone had broken in, he grabbed a wrench from his tool box and waited. He does not mind admitting that he felt quite fearful, but this feeling was to turn somewhat deeper when the footsteps stopped. Fully expecting the door to open, he prepared himself; but nothing happened. Slowly he made his way to the door and opened it. There was nobody there. The husband put on the lights and searched the house. He found all the windows and door secure and that he was, indeed, the only person in the property.

Unfortunately for his peace of mind, this happened several more times over the following months. The man, however, refused to believe in a paranormal explanation and put it down to the night creaking of an old house.

With the refurbishment complete, the family moved in and the guest house was once more open for business. Before long, the children started talking about feeling as though there was somebody in their bedroom and in later years, one friend who stayed the night was scared out of her wits at seeing an old tennis ball roll across the floor of its own accord. Another of the children's friends also saw a ball fall down the staircase towards her when there was no-one at the top to start it off.

In addition to all this, there were occasions when a strong smell of pipe tobacco would suddenly emanate in the first-floor front-middle bedroom. Old documents reveal that this room was once The Turks Head gaming room.

The building also had a couple of other interesting curiosities. While stripping off the wallpaper in one of the bedrooms that adjoined the Elim Church building to the right, a small door was discovered. It had obviously been papered over for many years, but opened without too much of a struggle to reveal a tiny room beyond. The only window of sorts in the room was a small square opening in the opposite wall. On further investigation it was discovered that the room was in fact the projector room of the old Belle Vue cinema, which occupied the building before it was taken over by the Elim Church in 1956. It seemed strange that the only access to the room was via a bedroom in the next-door lodging house!

When the family decided to replace the surface of their rear yard, they were amazed to discover the original cobbles underneath and still in a good state of repair. In addition to seeing these stones from the past, I'm told you could also still smell the horses; it was as if that distinctive aroma had unexplainably embedded itself in the cobbles.

Number 39

Formerly an nineteenth-century lodging house, the property has now been converted into two self-contained flats. During the summer of 1998, a young woman took up residence in the ground-floor apartment. Within a very short time, she sensed that she was being watched, and never more so than when she crossed the passageway separating the lounge and kitchen.

This 'L'-shaped passageway led from the living room to the rear garden-access door and a staircase down to the bedrooms. The young woman felt that whatever watched her, did so from the corner of the 'L', and there was often a distinct feeling of coldness, like a draught caught in the corner, which could be felt by visiting friends and family members as well as the young woman herself.

One particularly sunny day, when coming in through the garden door, she was very surprised to momentarily see what looked like the shadow of figure standing in the corner. The figure, however, disappeared very quickly and the young woman convinced herself that there was never any figure; it was merely her eyes adjusting from the bright outdoor light to the darker light of the passageway.

Several days later, she was once again coming in from the garden and again there was the fleeting glimpse of a figure standing in the corner. To accompany this glimpse, she noticed there also seemed a strange feeling of heaviness in the air, with the sensation particularly strong in the corner.

Nothing more was seen or felt for two months, until one evening, just as she was coming out of the kitchen, she looked down the passageway and was shocked to see an older woman standing in the corner smiling at her. The woman was dressed in a long, grey full skirt, a dark high-neck blouse and a white cap on top of her piled up hair. After what seemed to be many minutes, but was in reality only a few seconds, the smiling woman faded from view and was never seen again. From that day on, the cold spots and sense of being watched never occurred again.

The Cutter Hotel

Standing on the corner of East Street and St Alban Street, the ground floor of The Cutter gives the impression of being a rather compact, traditional wet pub, consisting only of a small bar room fronting onto East Street and a larger rear-bar reached via a side door on St Alban Street, or a small passageway between the rooms. However, upstairs is a different matter. The myriad of rooms reflects the true origins of the establishment, which was that of a large and busy steam-packet hotel.

The premises still offer rooms, but the importance of the business as a major hotel has now diminished. But it does seem that at least one former guest or bar worker was so taken with the place that they still pay regular visits from beyond the grave! Both locals and visitors enjoying a drink in the front bar have reported looking through into the rear room and spotting a female sitting up at the bar. Drinkers alert the bar staff that someone needs serving in there, but when the bar tender turns to walk through into the other area, the place where she was sitting is empty.

The woman is consistently described as blonde and attractive, and some have remarked that she is quite buxom too! Her age is a different matter; it has been judged as anything from late twenties to early forties. It's been difficult to ascertain the exact time period she hails from, as she does not appear to wear any distinctive clothing or item of fashion that could help to identify a particular era, and none of the older regulars remember anyone of her description having a close association with the hotel in their living memory. Similarly, no-one seems to have a clue as to why she should keep appearing at the rear bar. There is no record of any female deaths or murders at the property and, according to those who have seen her, she does not look distressed in any way, so it seems she had not suffered an event traumatic or upsetting enough to keep her spirit grounded. One suggestion is that she is a former landlady, still keeping a watchful eye over what was once her business, while another theory hints at the lady being engaged in a more dubious form of employment, perhaps frequenting the bar in order to meet 'clients'.

In addition to the unidentified blonde woman in the bar, a much older female has been spotted, the last time being October

The Cutter Hotel. Who is the buxom lady who waits at the bar?

2010. A regular saw an elderly woman, with greying hair in a bun and shoulders draped in a dark shawl, walk from the door behind the bar, which leads to the cellar and the landlord's accommodation, through the short lobby between the bars and out into St Alban street via the side door. The old woman has also been spotted sitting in the corner of the rear bar and smoking a clay pipe. The census of 1851 shows the landlord to be James Sly, who lived on the premises with his wife Harriet and his seventy-three-year-old mother Sarah. Could the sightings of an older woman be the spirit of Sarah, walking and smoking in death the same as she did in life?

While the sightings of long-dead visitors or occupants can be a little disturbing, whatever is residing in the cellar seems to be the cause of disruption in the flow of beer -- and that is not good as far as those serving and drinking are concerned! Bar staff often find that halfway through pouring a drink the gas runs out. However, when they go into the cellar to investigate, they find the gas taps have been turned off. Sometimes the taps will be turned off straight after they have been turned back on, resulting in staff yo-yoing between bar and cellar until either they or the mischievous spirit tire of the exercise. New barrels are also moved around at random.

Although the present landlord and his family have only experienced quite benign activity, a previous occupant was not so lucky. He claims to have always felt very uneasy in the cellar and in several of the upstairs rooms. This feeling culminated in an incident of almost actual physical harm when, one day, as he was leaning out of a bathroom window in order to paint the frame, he felt himself suddenly being pushed from behind. Thinking quickly, he dropped the paint tin and brush and grabbed the frame. The pushing became stronger and he eventually had to hold on with all of his strength until the force subsided.

Hell Lane

Renamed Helen Lane (sometimes spelt Hellen) in the nineteenth century, the clean and respectable houses that stand there today belie its former name, which was thought to originate from the fact that the street and its inhabitants were the first to encounter the ravages of the Plague.

In June 1348, a ship bearing a Plague-stricken Frenchman from Gascony docked at the port of Melcombe Regis. The poor man was taken into one of the nearby cottages and a priest from Radipole sent for. The man died and, before long, every occupant of the cottage and those adjoining it suffered the same fate. The Black Death spread with speed along the lane, and such was the misery and suffering of all those living there that it gained the reputation of being a living 'Hell'.

Today, nothing remains of the houses of 1348, but on still evenings it is claimed that you can hear the soft cries and moans of those dying from this most horrendous disease. On one of our walks we were accompanied by a visiting medium, who, on entering the lane, claimed to suddenly feel an overwhelming sense of sadness and heaviness. Nothing of the lane's history was revealed beforehand and the medium was from the north of England.

The Clipper

The public house now known as The Clipper started life as the rectory for the Reverend of Melcombe Regis. A part of

the building ended up being incorporated into the new Jubilee Hall, which became a cinema and eventually a modern-day bingo hall. During the 1989 redevelopment of this part of St Thomas Street, the remains of the Jubilee Hall, along with the bingo hall, were being demolished when parts of the forgotten rectory were discovered. It was decided to restore the rectory to its former glory and include it in the redevelopment plan. Surrounding properties were duly purchased, but problems with the developers meant a long delay before work started, and the whole block fell victim to vandalism and decay.

Eventually the redevelopment took place and the building opened as the Old Rectory public house. Almost from the start, the pub gained a reputation for unu-

sual and strange happenings. Doors would open and close by themselves in both public and private areas, and footsteps could be heard after closing time on a staircase leading down to the cellar.

One of the most concentrated active areas was the downstairs ladies' toilets. A number of women have reported the unsettling feeling of being watched, while others consider the place to have a brooding and nasty atmosphere. A few unlucky ladies have also had the unfortunate experience of being fleetingly touched by an unseen hand while 'going about their business'.

The business was later to become The Barracuda Bar and following a further period of refurbishment it is now know as The Clipper.

Shortly after reopening under its present name, staff began to notice an ever-increasing level of unexplained happenings. Among the most common events were beer pumps suddenly running dry and the door to the newly created upstairs ladies' toilet opening and closing on its own. This door can be easily seen by those working behind the bar, and most of the staff have witnessed the occurrence. One of the more frequent and inconvenient happenings is the sudden loss of electrical power. Such was the problem that electricians were called in to identify, and hopefully rectify, the cause. Unfortunately, no cause was found; everything to do with the wiring and supply was exactly as it should be.

Slightly less inconvenient, but just as unwelcome, is when people have put an item down, only to discover moments later that it has either gone or moved to a different place. This happens to some degree all over the building, and while some occurrences could be put down to other occupants or staff moving an object to another place or putting something away, it is hard to use this explanation when you are alone in the cellar. The manageress confesses that she dislikes the cellar but, of course, has to go in there to do her job. One day, she was doing a quick stock check and put down her clipboard and pen on top of a crate of bottles so she could use both hands to move some boxes. When she turned back to pick up the clipboard it was not there. Searching all over the cellar, she eventually discovered the items back on the crate, exactly where she had left them! The manageress was absolutely certain she was on her own and that no other member of staff had come down to the cellar, as she would have heard them on the staircase.

The Clipper, originally the rectory for the Reverend of Weymouth.

The manageress also reports that she frequently hears unexplained footsteps moving around the top-floor flat that she shares with her boyfriend.

A number of reasons for the paranormal happenings have been put forward. One is that the brooding and unfriendly atmosphere in the downstairs ladies' toilets comes from the time when the terrace was boarded up, waiting redevelopment. A tramp, looking for a place to sleep out of the cold, found his way into the basement of the hidden rectory and sadly passed away in that spot. His body was not found until the redevelopment began. I have been unable to discover if there is any truth to this, as I cannot find any official reports or newspaper articles to verify a body being found.

The most enduring theory given for the disturbances in the cellar and bar is that the rector haunts the premises, showing displeasure that his former home is now a place where alcohol is served and consumed.

I have also, in the course of writing this book, spoken to a former employee of the cinema that once existed on this site, who tells me that when she worked there as a young usherette, items in the upstairs office and projection room would go missing and inexplicably reappear elsewhere. Along with other girls who worked there, she really disliked being on her own in the office and felt that the place had a 'strange atmosphere'.

The Black Dog

Just as The Boot lays claim to being the oldest and the most haunted pub in Weymouth, The Black Dog is a strong contender for both of those titles on the Melcombe Regis side.

A large part of the building dates back to the sixteenth century and is one of the few 'Saxon Frame' buildings remaining in the UK. It was formerly known as The Dove, until the town won the contract to trade with the new British colonies of Newfoundland and Labrador. The landlord of that time purchased a black Newfoundland Labrador dog from one of the new trading ships in that region and, as the breed was one of the first to be seen in the South West, it attracted at lot of attention, with curious people coming from miles around to view the animal and, of course, have a drink or two while they were there. In honour of his dog, and the prosperity its arrival had brought him, the landlord changed the pub's name to the one it bears today.

For a great number of years, almost every form of paranormal activity has been experienced in the building, both by landlords and members of the public. One of the most intriguing are the various different smells that seem to linger on the staircase, close to what is now the kitchen.

While food is served at lunchtimes, the kitchen is closed in the evenings, and yet the aroma of a hearty stew cooking is often smelt when passing along the nearby landing on one's way up or down the staircase. Quite recently, for a period of around three weeks, the unmistakable smell of an old-fashioned 'Valor' paraffin heater was very noticeable in the same place. The smoke of strong pipe tobacco and cigars are smelt both on the staircase and throughout the bar area. Needless to say, there are no paraffin heaters kept on the premises and, although reports of tobacco smells predate the smoking ban, it is hard to explain the occurrences reported since this law came into force. One of the most curious smells is that of burning or burnt candles. This particular smell happens all over the building, in both public and private areas. Being a very pungent and distinctive smell, it has caused many to comment as they walk into the bar.

While there seems to be no known reason for most of the smells, there is a link to the candle aroma. The English Civil War was raging, and during the siege of Melcombe in February 1645, a trader named as William Courtney, from Taunton Dene, lodged at The Black Dog (then known as 'a house of entertainment'). One night, as William slept, the landlord, John Chiles, battered him on the forehead with a hammer, in order to steal the £288 in gold and the £12 in silver that William was carrying with him. Chiles and his wife, Margaret, stripped the body and then put a lighted candle in an upstairs window to signal to outside accomplices to come and help them dispose of the body. In the darkness, William's remains were taken to a nearby jetty and thrown into the sea. The murderous pair hoped that one more bloodied body found in a war zone, at a time when death was commonplace, would not raise suspicion. Unfortunately for them, these hopes were dashed when William's body was recognised and identified as one of their lodgers. Both Chiles and his wife were arrested, questioned and tried for murder.

The building saw a second murder in 1758, when it was a haunt for smugglers who operated along the south coast. An argument occurred one night between John 'Smoaker' Mills senior, Richard Mills and Richard Hawkins. Both of the Mills were members of the infamous Hawkhurst smuggling gang from Sussex, and they accused Hawkins of an offence against the gang. Words soon turned to violence and Hawkins was whipped to death by the two men, in front of the fireplace that now stands in the rear of the bar area. The murderers were caught and later hanged for their crime. It was also later found that Hawkins was entirely innocent of the accusations made against him.

This well-documented story may explain the sightings of a ghostly fight that has been seen on several occasions near to the fireplace. Witnesses who have come across the scene describe it as two men, dressed in rough shirts and leather jerkins, bearing down upon a third man, who falls to the floor; the trio then fade from view.

A good friend of the present-day licensees has also experienced paranormal activity here. The gentleman, who is a retired policeman, along with his wife, was staying on the premises for a short holiday. One morning, the friend opened the door onto the upstairs passageway and a gentleman in a trilby hat passed by and headed downstairs. Thinking it was another guest, he took no notice and shortly afterwards took a similar path. However, noticing the trilby-wearing man was not downstairs, he asked who the man was. The landlord replied that he did not have any other guests staying in the building. Despite assurances that there was no man in a trilby in the building, the friend remained positive of what he had seen.

A few days later, however, a regular of the pub dropped by with a copy of a newspaper article from the 1960s, which reported the death of a longstanding landlord of The Black Dog. Coincidentally, the accompanying photo showed a man wearing a trilby hat. The landlord showed it to his friend, who was amazed to see it was the same man who had passed him in the passageway a few days earlier.

To add to sightings of a long-dead landlord, murderous smugglers and their victim, the landlord's daughter has glimpsed the shadowy figure of a female in some of the upstairs rooms.

The Black Dog, Melcome Regis' oldest inn, and the scene of two violent murders.

Inside The Black Dog. It is in front of the fireplace that a ghostly replay of the savage whipping of Richard Hawkins has been seen.

Although two grisly murders have taken place, the present landlord reports that none of the happenings seem malicious or particularly nasty; he describes them more as playful occurrences, albeit a little annoying or frustrating on occasions.

One evening, just before retiring to bed, the landlord heard the sound of the automatic room freshener. The device was set to spray once every thirty minutes, but on this occasion it continued to spray some fifteen times, until the landlord shouted, 'I know you are there now please stop!' Miraculously, it did.

Overnight guests frequently feel their hair being gently tugged or their shoulders shaken as they lie in bed. One guest, who wore an eye mask, woke up to hear a voice saying 'hello'. Terrified that someone had broken into his room, he quickly took off the mask, only to find the room empty except for himself. The landlord and landlady have had similar experiences, in addition to hearing footsteps coming up the stairs and along the passageway outside their room when they know themselves to be the only occupants in the building.

The landlady has a strong dislike for toilet lids being left up, and her husband is careful to make sure that he always leaves the lid down after paying a visit to the facilities in their private accommodation. Annoyingly, however, some unseen hand mischievously lifts the lid back up. The landlord insists that he is not using a story of a loo-lid-lifting ghost as an excuse for his own forgetfulness, and his wife has encountered a similar phenomenon also.

Although the landlord and landlady knew the pub had a history of alleged paranormal activity, it was still a bit of a shock when one night, very shortly after moving in, they heard an enormous crash in the room above them. They suspected that unpacked boxes of their possessions had fallen over, as following the crash the ceiling light-fitting seemed to swing, just as it would if something had heavily hit the floor above. The pair went upstairs to assess the damage and found that all the boxes were in exactly the same place as they had been left; nothing had fallen.

Very soon afterwards, the landlord became convinced someone was living in the roof space, as things were going missing, never to be seen again or turning up in odd places, and they regularly heard someone, or something, moving about up there. Eventually he managed to gain access to the roof space, but found nothing amiss and no signs of human habitation.

Whoever is haunting The Black Dog seems to also have an affect on more technical aspects of the premises. There have been several periods when any item containing a printed circuit board would malfunction. Fruit machines from a local supplier would work perfectly well in their workshop, only to fail less than twenty-four hours later, for no apparent reason, when sited in the pub. A coffee machine used in the bar stopped working so many times that eventually it had to be replaced by one that did not contain any circuit boards.

Lights switching themselves on and off led to the landlord calling in an electrician to check the wiring. Interestingly, when the power had been completely shut off, one lightbulb started to emit a faint pulsating glow which continued until the power was put back on.

Engineers had to be called in when one evening, approximately ninety minutes into service, the intruder alarms were activated, even though they were switched off. As the controls were already set in the 'off' position, the only thing that could be done was to wait for the internal battery to wear down, which made for a noisy time. Once the batteries had flattened, peace was not permanently restored; only a matter of moments later the fire alarms went off! The following day, an engineer opened up the control box, which is situated on a wall just inside the passageway leading from the bar to the stairs. He found the inside of the box to be wet and asked the landlord if there had been any sort of leak recently to account for water getting onto the box. The landlord replied that there had been no leaks either above the box or indeed anywhere else in the pub, as the wall on which the box is positioned was perfectly dry, just like the low ceiling above it.

More traditional poltergeist activity comes in the form of books flying off shelves in the bar and landing several feet away, much to the amazement of those standing nearby. One time, a group of people were discussing the Civil War Crabchurch Conspiracy, and the book of the same title landed at their feet. Destructive activity is thankfully rare, but on one occasion a line of glasses was swept off the bar top and onto the floor. This was witnessed by the landlord and a member of the bar staff.

At some time prior to the present landlord taking over the lease, the decision was taken to lower the floor in the cellar, as the headroom in there was very restrictive and it was not possible to raise the ceiling. As the floor was dug out, several boxes were discovered buried in the soil under the floor. Inside, wrapped in oiled skins, were flintlock muskets. The muskets were in perfect condition and now reside in Weymouth Museum. A more blood-curdling find was the human remains buried in what seemed to be a fallen-in tunnel that once led off in a seaward direction. A second tunnel was also discovered and this one seemed to lead off at a 90-degree angle towards the ridge of land where King George III had his seaside residence. The discovery of this tunnel added credence to the local tale of the King having a secret passage built from his lodge to The Black Dog, so he could visit undetected and take advantage of the female pleasures to be had there!

The landlord commented that the sightings near the fireplace of men fighting are simply an unearthly recording of a tragic event; the replaying is triggered periodically by an unknown source but, in addition to this, he also believes there are at least two male, one female and two very young spirits present. At the time it was built, The Black Dog would have been virtually on the beach, and parts of the building have been found to contain timbers from old ships. One of the upper rooms is floored with deck planks and the landlord has suggested that some of the spirits might be linked with one of the ships that donated building or flooring timbers.

Note: While interviewing the landlord and landlady in these premises, the necklace I had worn for most of the day somehow became unclasped and dropped to the floor. The clasp is a type known as a lobster claw, which requires someone to pull down on the catch in order to open it. On checking the necklace, I found that the clasp was intact and the only way the necklace could have fallen was by someone physically opening the clasp. Needless to say, there was no-one to be seen behind me at the time!

The Golden Lion

A former eighteenth-century coaching inn, situated on the corner of St Mary Street and St Edmund Street, is reputed to have at least three ghosts. The majority of sightings are of two ladies who seem to wander at will through the upper rooms. An old man, believed to be a fisherman, has also been spotted several times sitting at the end of the bar, while a group of phantom ladies are reputed to be whiling away eternity, playing card games at a table in the corner of the main bar. Sounds of whispering and muffled laughter have also been heard coming from the small courtyard to the rear of the building when the gates have been locked and no-one in the area at the time.

The Cannonball House

Positioned on the corner of Maiden Street and St Edmund Street, the building is well known amongst locals and visitors for having a Civil War cannonball firmly lodged in the stonework beneath one of the upper windows.

The ground floor of the building now serves as public conveniences, but in the 1790s it was a butcher's shop belonging to a tradesman by the name of Rudge. Above the shop lived Rudge, his wife and children, and a servant called Margery. Not long after the family had moved in, Margery asked her master who the old lady in the red shawl was, as she had seen her in the house several times during the very early or late hours of the day. Rudge replied that the description seemed to belong to that of his late great-grandmother, of whom he had a painting.

The Golden Lion.

When he showed the picture to Margery, she exclaimed that it was definitely the same old woman she had seen. Rudge rebuked her, saying she must have imagined it and that she was not to say anything to his wife who was with child and not well. Margery kept to her word, but continued to see the old woman; however, another member of the household was soon to share the sightings.

Following the birth of her fourth child, Mrs Rudge lay half awake in bed, when through the chink in the heavy four-poster curtains, she glimpsed the figure of a woman pass by. Thinking it was the nurse, she was quite alarmed to discover an elderly lady looking at her through the curtains. Noted for wearing a red shawl, the

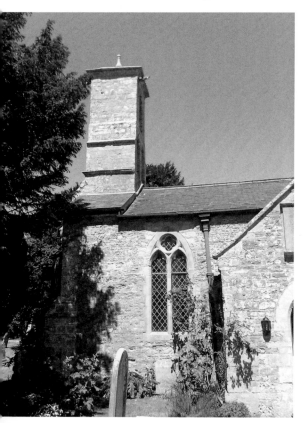

St Ann at Radipole, where the body discovered in the hidden room was finally laid to rest.

old woman raised her arm to point at the opposite wall and then faded from view.

When told of her experience, Rudge and the nurse brushed it off as simply a dream. Mrs Rudge accepted this explanation, but it became very much harder to accept when she continued to be visited by the old woman in the red shawl, who always, before disappearing, pointed to the wall. Convinced that these continued sightings could not be a dream, and that the old woman was trying to tell her something, Mrs Rudge spoke to her husband and demanded that the wall be taken down, as she strongly felt that something was hidden behind it.

Although not entirely convinced, such was his wife's conviction that Rudge sought the help of a family member who was a respected builder. The builder examined the east wall and proceeded to take it apart. To everyone's surprise, there was indeed something behind the wall. It was a doorway that had been plastered over, and upon freeing the lock, it opened to reveal a small windowless room.

Inside there was a stool, upon which lay a felt hat of a long-past style, and the floor was strewn with old documents and parchments. In the corner there was a long, large wooden box. The two men lifted the lid, thinking that they had found a secret horde of family silver, reputed to have been lost in the Civil War. They were horrified to discover instead the skeletal remains of what appeared to be a man.

The skeleton was still clad in armour and it was plain to see from the state of his skull that he had died from serious head wounds. With everyone wondering who the poor fellow was, Mr Rudge remembered that his great-grandparents used to live in the house during the Civil War, and he had been told by his grandmother that her

FEES PAYABLE TO THE RECTOR OF RADIPOLE

BURIALS	£.s.d	MARRIAGES	£.s.d
Each Funeral	.1.	By Licence	1.1.
For breaking the ground when first of a family (extra) }	.6.8	By Banns	.5.
		Publication of Banns	.2.6
For a nonparishioner (extra)	1.1.	Certificate of Register	.2.6
Vault for one	5.5.		
Any Vault which will take two is charged as a Vault for Two }	10.10	The Churching of Women each	.1.
Vault for two	10.10.	**CLERKS FEES**	
Reopening a Vault	2.2.	Making each grave	.7.
Permission to place a Headstone	5.5.	Making vault for one	1.1.
Permission to place a Footstone	.10.6	Making vault for two	
Extra inscription on a Head=stone	.10.6	Reopening a vault	.10.6
		Placing a Headstone or Footstone	.2.6
		Extra inscription on a Headstone	.2.6
Railing, Tombstone, or enclosure }	5.5.	Railing, Tombstone, or enclosure	1.1.
		Marriage By Licence	.10.6
		Marriage By Banns	.2.6
		Publication of Banns	.1.

Church fees on display in the porch at St Ann's.

father had fought for King Charles. Sadly, he had fallen during the battle to take the town, and it was thought that the victorious Roundheads had thrown all the bodies, her father's included, into the sea.

Rudge speculated that the remains were those of this great-grandfather, whose body had instead been brought back to the house to rest for eternity, hidden away from Roundhead hands behind a walled-up door. It was decided that the discovery should, for now, be kept secret, and the poor fellow should at last receive a Christian burial. Very early one morning, the man was quietly interred, alongside others from his family, in the churchyard of St Ann at Radipole.

The hidden room was cleaned and a window put in to create a dressing room for the master bedroom. The felt hat fell to pieces when touched, and the document and parchments were found to contain nothing of any great value and were used by Mrs Rudge to cover her jars of pickles and preserves! There is no mention of anyone ever again seeing the ghostly old woman in the red shawl, so it was assumed that with her mission accomplished, she too could rest in peace.

Dolce Vita

Some years ago, No. 62 St Thomas Street was the Weymouth branch of former bank chain TSB. For the past decade, it has been occupied by a variety of bars providing food and late-night entertainment; its latest incarnation is Dolce Vita.

Back in 2001, it first opened doors to the public as The Toad @ The Bank, in honour of its previous function. It was at this time that a few strange occurrences started.

On one occasion, a member of staff was making her way from the cellar area into the adjacent bar and dropped a complete tray of freshly cleaned glasses. When a colleague came to her aid and asked what had happened, she replied that she had been grabbed on both sides of her waist, which had startled her and caused her to drop the glasses.

That same year, a number of staff members had finished for the night and had decided to sit beside one of the windows at the front of the bar. All staff were present when the phone rang. This doesn't sound unusual at first, but in fact it was an internal phone that was ringing; yet all of the people that had worked that night were sat in the same group, with everyone accounted for. The rest of the building was closed and empty. You have to ask: who made that call?

The Lone Sea Mistress of Newtons Cove

Behind Brewers Quay at Newtons Cove, just as you step on to the bridge that takes you to Bincleaves Road, sits a small hut that serves ice-creams and teas during the summer months. It is at this place that the ghostly mistress of a seaman who was lost at sea stands alone and looks out for her beloved. She is thought to be distraughtly waving her arms for him to come back into the shore.

The Town Bridge

Witnessed by many people over the years, a dark figure of a man in a brown cloak is seen rowing a wooden boat under the bridge, but he never emerges on the other side.

Bincome Railway Tunnel

The main line from Weymouth to Dorchester runs through a deep tunnel, cut through the hillside on the northern out-skirts of Weymouth. Bincombe tunnel was opened in the late 1850s and has long held a reputation for being haunted.

It is a sad fact that countless numbers of unfortunate or unhappy people have met their deaths on railways. While these tragic events occur nationwide, reports seem to imply that in the early years of railway operation, there was a higher than average number of both accidental and deliberate deaths in Bincombe tunnel – so much so that the place was once christened the 'tunnel of ill repute'.

In 1987, the tunnel's reputation struck again when a commuter, who thought he had missed his last train home, decided to walk along the track from Upwey station to Dorchester, as it offered the shortest route and avoided the long uphill walk over Ridgeway Hill. Unfortunately, his train was running late and he was killed in Bincombe tunnel.

Shortly afterwards in 1991, no less than four incidences of unexplainable happenings were reported by train drivers. One driver had seen what appeared to have been a ghostly figure in the tunnel. The driver said after his experience, 'I distinctly remember seeing someone walking towards the train. There was nothing I could do and the train must have gone straight through him! Yet there was nothing resembling human remains ever found!'

Another train driver told of a very similar story, although he was unaware at the time that anything of the kind had been reported before. He said, ' I was approaching the Bincombe tunnel stretch of line that has become very familiar to me, when I thought I saw something in the mouth of the tunnel. The next moment, I could make out the shape of a man and he was just standing there as the train raced towards him. His clothes may have been rather old fashioned, but I was amazed that he didn't

Newtons Cove. The new promenade obliterates the former rocky inlet and beach where smugglers landed their booty and a weeping mistress awaited the return of her lover.

Town Bridge. Who is the man in the boat that disappears under the bridge?

55

attempt to get out of the way. I closed my eyes and it was all over – nothing! I reported the incident but nothing was found, nothing at all, but I know what I saw.'

Other experienced and long-serving train drivers have reported sounds that they have been unable to explain. One said he was just approaching the Bincombe tunnel when he 'heard this thumping and crashing that seemed to be coming from the outside of the train, but there was nothing to account for it.' He added, 'It was completely unfathomable.' Yet another driver has said, 'I had heard odd noises and seen strange shapes on the line – and usually on a Friday night. That night there is often lots of thumping and banging all the way through the tunnel.'

A regular commuter on the line has also reported inexplicable sounds, but very different ones from those reported by the train drivers, and apparently originating from in the train itself. As the train entered the tunnel, the commuter heard what sounded like moaning and whisperings coming from one of the toilets. The noises stopped when the train emerged from the tunnel and the commuter was astonished to see the toilet door swing open and no-one come out.

The Ghost Ship

Over the years, there have been many sightings of a ship with a tall mast, in full sail, heading into Weymouth Bay, which then eerily fades into thin air.

Modern-day and preserved 'tall ships' do frequent the area on a regular basis and, no doubt, account for some of the sightings, especially in misty or hazy conditions, but several independent witnesses have described the ship as being larger than the type usually seen in the harbour, and one witness in particular was shocked to

Bincombe railway tunnel.

Weymouth Bay and Melcome Regis sands, as viewed from the Weymouth side of the harbour.

see a picture of the exact same ship on dis-play in Weymouth Museum.

The ship in the picture was the *Earl of Abergavenny*, an 'East Indianman' built in 1797 and captained by John Wordsworth, brother of the poet William.

On the night of 5 February 1805, the Earl of Abergavenny was making for Bengal and China, when during bad weather she struck the Shambles bank, just off Portland Bill. Although the crew eventually managed to free the ship, she was badly damaged and taking in water fast. The captain decided to head for the somewhat calmer waters of Weymouth Bay and perhaps make an attempt to beach the vessel. Unfortunately, she never made it; she sank a little over two miles from safety, resulting in the drowning of around 250 crew and passengers, includ-ing John Wordsworth.

Melcombe Villa

Melcombe Villa is a small guesthouse, standing proudly behind the summer resi-dence of King George III and adjoining the quirky Turton Villa, once home to Dr John Turton, King George's personal physician.

The previous owners have reported that the house held a happy and warm atmos-phere for the majority of the day. However, this changed between 9.30 p.m. and 10 p.m. each evening, when a shadowy figure would walk along the ground-floor corridor, past the kitchen and out of the door. Around five to ten minutes later, the figure would make the return journey. At first, the owner assumed it was one of their guests taking a pre-bed stroll, but the figure continued to be seen when there were no guests in residence. The figure appeared almost every evening for the nineteen years the owners lived in the building, and it never once varied in either its timing or its path; neither did it speak or acknowledge anyone watching.

Christopher Robin

Situated on the Esplanade, the building was once a grand house belonging to the Earl of Wilton's estate. Nowadays, it is better known as Weymouth's longest established fancy-dress and goods shop, with the rooms upstairs converted to holiday flats. Visitors to the shop, or those staying in any of the flats, need not worry about experiencing any paranormal encounters, however, as according to the present owner, these seemed to only occur below the stairs in the warren of basement rooms, which now serve to hold the shop stock.

As you descend down the wooden staircase, one surviving servants' bell on the wall serves as a reminder that this was once a residential property of some note. Nineteenth-century census records list the household staff to be as many as eight, which included a groom and a footman.

For at least twenty years, shop staff have felt a watching presence when they have been working in the basement, and at times this feeling has been so intense that they have turned round expecting to find that a co-worker had joined them.

Behind an old wooden door, to the front of the basement, are what appear to be two small tunnels. It has been discovered that they were in fact an underground coal bunker and a cold store, which, when the house was built, would have been accessible from either the servants' or tradesmen's entrance down an outside flight of steps, which at some point in the past was cov-

Christopher Robin, the fancy-dress shop where unseen eyes keep watch in the basement.

ered over to make a direct and level access into the shop. Nowadays, these tunnels are used to also house spare shop fittings and little-used items. On occasions when staff have had to go into this area, they have felt very uneasy for no particular reason and, again, have experienced the strong feeling that they are not alone.

A few times, a figure moving about the storage area has been glimpsed by a staff member enjoying a tea break near the back door, but when called out to, the figure does not respond and instead disappears.

It has also been reported that items stacked securely on the storage racks will suddenly fall onto the floor, sometimes landing at a distance greater than one would expect if they had simply slipped off the shelf.

Duke of Albany

Situated towards the far end Park Street, the Duke of Albany is a traditional corner pub where you can find a friendly welcome and an excellent pint. There's a pool table and a fruit machine for entertainment, and sometimes customers are treated to a little paranormal entertainment too! Strange, unexplained happenings have become so frequent and numerous that the landlords, bar staff and their regulars consider them almost normal.

In the main bar area, it has been known for glasses to raise themselves up off a shelf and seemingly float unaided in mid-air, before settling back down in their place. Glasses have also been seen to move off the shelf, as if held by an unseen hand, and fall gently to the floor; so gently in fact that these glasses never break.

Boxes of games that are securely stored above the bar on deep shelves have inexplicably fallen to the floor, and it is quite usual to suddenly experience extreme icy cold spots in the bar, snug and rear storeroom.

For a long period, bar staff and landlords found their beer pumps to run dry and gases turned off for no reason. The problem was identified by a visiting medium, who explained that a previous, and now deceased, landlady disapproved of the beer they were serving!

The late landlady, or maybe another spirit, does approve of whatever the landlord drinks though, as on one occasion the phantom stole his glass. It was a quiet lunchtime and the landlord was in front of the bar, chatting to his only customer, who was sat near to the front window. The landlord placed his glass on the bar behind him and when he went to take another drink,

The Duke of Albany. A former landlady makes her opinion in regards to the beer that is served.

it had completely disappeared. Although he looked all round to see if he had mistakenly placed his half-empty glass somewhere else, or if it had somehow fallen on the floor behind the bar, no trace of the glass was to be found, and as his wife was out and none of his bar staff on duty, he had no explanation of what happened to his drink.

The medium has identified another spirit; one of a man who walks through the upper bedrooms and landlord's living quarters.

Cobham Drive

Situated between Chickerell Road and Radipole Lane, Cobham Drive is part of a social housing estate built upon the old Weymouth Airfield. It takes it name from a famous flying circus that performed there in the early 1930s. With war loom-ing, the airfield was requisitioned and RAF Chickerell came into operation. Although the entire airfield was built upon after it was returned to civilian use in 1959, the edging stones of the entrance to the camp can still be seen today.

Early one summer morning in the late 1980s, just after daybreak, a resident prepared to leave her house for an early shift at a factory on the nearby Granby Estate. On drawing back the curtains to the rear of her house, she was horrified to see the distinct figure of a man at the bottom of her garden. He had his head bowed down towards the ground and seemed to be searching for something. The woman woke her husband, but when he joined her at the window the man had gone. The husband accused his wife of seeing things, but she was quite sure that she had witnessed someone and, although it was not light

All that remains of RAF Chickerell is the bell-mouthed entrance, which is nowadays mistaken for a lay-by along the busy Radipole Lane.

enough to see the man's features, she could see he was wearing a light-coloured great-coat with a belt.

The following month, at around the same time of day, a neighbour was out watering his plants when he too noticed the figure of a man standing at the bottom of a garden a few houses along. The neighbour could see that he was not one of the occupants whom he knew well and, worried that the person was up to no good, he shouted at him to be off. The figure did not respond; instead he bent down as if to look at the ground. The neighbour shouted again, before realising that the man seemed to have vanished into thin air.

The incident played on the neighbour's mind and, although not wanting to appear stupid or fanciful, he decided to tell the householder whose garden the man had been standing in what he had seen. The neighbours were intrigued to discover that they had both seen the same man but on different occasions. They agreed that he was wearing a light-coloured greatcoat with a belt, and that he seemed to be looking on the ground for something before he disappeared.

The man was never seen again to their knowledge, and the incident was forgotten about until an article appeared in the local paper a number of years later about RAF Chickerell. The article included a picture of airmen in uniform and one of them was wearing a greatcoat exactly the same as the man in the garden.

Was the figure the spirit of an airman, not able to rest until finding whatever he was looking for, or was it simply a living person dressed against the early morning chill in an ex-RAF greatcoat, the type of which can be bought in military surplus shops? If the latter is true, then just one question remains: how did he manage to leave the gardens in the blink of an eye?

Abbotsbury Road

In 2006, an unassuming terrace house along Abbotsbury Road was undergoing reno-vation. The building was found to have a possible link to the poltergeist activity that the owner and her family had been experiencing.

A decorator had finally stripped off the last of several layers of wallpaper and uncovered a mural painted directly onto the original lime-plaster walls of the dining room. The painting is around 5ft wide by 4ft high and depicts three galleons and a small boat containing a group of dark-skinned men. The boats are surrounded by sky, clouds and sea, and a possible theory is that it is a representation of the capture of three Spanish Armada galleons. It was also thought that the painting could date back to when the house was built in 1881, when it was owned by a station master called John Palmer. Some parts of the mural are unfin-ished though, and sketched pencil lines can be clearly seen. A further unfinished paint-ing was discovered on the chimney breast in the same room.

Prior to the mural's discovery, lights and TVs would come on and switch off on their own. Things would routinely go missing and the younger children of the house would wake up crying and unset-tled, complaining about a man in the room. Sometimes they would talk about another man who brought them toys. The older children described the house, especially the upstairs front bedroom, as creepy, with intense cold spots that would come and go. On occasions, a shadow would be glimpsed moving from the back room to the kitchen, and there was frequently the sound of footsteps on the staircase and in the rooms above the living areas. The owner described it as sounding like someone else was in the house, but she knew she was alone.

Roman Ghosts

The figure of a man and a timid looking woman were seen at the top of the stairs, and a man was also spotted standing behind the owner in the hair salon she operated from the front ground-floor of the house.

Following the sighting of the man, the house owner asked a medium to visit the property and the spirit of a man was identified. The spirit was allegedly quite bossy and authoritative; he demanded the present owner got the house tied up and renovated.

Doing as the ghost had bid, she engaged builders and decorators, and this led to the painting being found.

The house owner reported that since the discovery of the mural, the paranormal activity continues but to a lesser degree, and often there is no activity at all for long periods.

Weymouth was used by the Romans as a port to service their large encampment at Dorchester, and there are several tales of ghostly Romans being sighted in and around the town.

One of the most enduring legends is that of a phantom legion of Roman soldiers marching along a disused stretch of track (formerly the old Roman road that runs parallel to the A354 at Ridgeway Hill), between the two towns. According to the legend, they are supposed to appear in times of national crisis.

The upper reaches of what is now Radipole Lake was used by the Romans as a port to land men, goods and supplies for their large encampment at Dorchester. Roman coins and remains of pottery have been found around the banks, along with the ghost of a lone Roman soldier. The solitary solider also makes an appearance further inland and has been spotted several times following a path that would nowadays lead along the alleyway between Debenhams and TK Maxx. Much to the alarm of the landlord at the time, the soldier was seen continuing his walk through the bar of The White Hart and out through the window fronting onto St Nicholas Street, before finally fading from view.

Goldfingers – Cellar Bar

New street is now little more than a narrow roadway existing, for the most part, to serve the rear entrance to properties and businesses fronting onto the Esplanade.

This was not the case in the late 1800s, when it was a commercially busy and densely populated street. One building of note still proudly displays the name 'Baxter', carved in stone across the roof façade. The name refers to Robert Baxter, who is listed in the census of 1861 as a merchant of ale and porter, whose business was housed in the building. In testament to his trade, a carved head of what could be the god Dionysus or Bacchus sits on the wall above the double-fronted doorway.

In the twentieth century Baxter's, as it became known, was used as a wine bar and a nightclub; today it is a lap-dancing club. In addition to the main door, there are two

The route of a lone Roman solider.

smaller doors to either side and it is the one leading to the Cellar Bar that is of interest.

From the mid-1960s to the present day, doormen and bar staff have reported an uneasy feeling when alone in the underground bar area. To make matters worse, sobs and cries of an unseen female can be heard. Such was the Cellar Bar's reputation for being haunted that one former employee, at the time when it was a nightclub, has told of bets regularly being taken amongst the doormen to see who could stay in the place the longest on their own after closing time. Apparently, some did not make it through to the end of one hour, but others, allegedly helped by more than a few glasses of Dutch courage, lasted longer.

It seems to be common knowledge locally that a murder of a woman took place on the premises, but these reports range in dates from the late nineteenth century up

Goldfingers, originally built to house an ale and porter merchant. Its modern-day Cellar Bar is now home to a distressed spirit.

to the early 1900s. The victim was either a young servant girl or a 'woman of easy virtue'. Does the poor woman still bemoan her fate, and is it her cries that make the legs of strong doormen tremble in fear?

It has been revealed, very recently, that a male cleaner refuses to go into the Cellar Bar after his experience working alone in there after closing time one evening.

Harbinger Hag

This tale is enough to ensure that no matter how tired your feet, you will not risk sitting down along the Esplanade.

On a very hot summer's day, a young man was walking with his fiancée. As they passed by one of the shelters containing wooden benches on the Esplanade, the young man suddenly felt an ice-cold feeling come over him and he noticed a strange

The carved head of Dionysus or Bacchus bears testament to the building's former and present occupation.

smell, which he later described as a combination of sulphur and decomposition. His eyes were drawn to the people sitting on the bench, and he caught the face of an old woman who was seated in the corner. She gave him a diabolical glance full of malignancy.

His fiancée's voice calling to him to catch up broke the spell, and the couple walked on to the end of the Esplanade. He suggested they make their way home by the road, but his fiancée wanted to return via the Esplanade and maybe to stop and sit there for a while. Happily they retraced their steps, but before long the man realised they were approaching the shelter where he had seen the horrid old woman.

Once again, he felt the same icy coldness and smelt the vile stench. The old woman was still sitting there and he was horrified when his fiancée made for the seat. He grabbed his girl and held her fast, begging her not to sit there.

The fiancée angrily threw off the man's hands, exclaiming that he was either mad, blind or both. The seat was empty and she was going to sit in it. The last thing he remembered was the old lady holding out her arms invitingly to his fiancée and watching as she sank into them with a sigh of relief.

The next thing the young man remembers is finding himself flat on the ground with a crowd gathered around him. Someone spoke to him in a kindly voice, saying he (the man) must have fainted in shock. When the man enquired about what sort of shock he had supposedly suffered, he was told that, unfortunately, as soon as his fiancée had sat down she'd suffered a heart attack and died.

Bibi's

The building dates from the Tudor period and is thought to be the last part of the medieval friary, which occupied a good proportion of the area around St Albans Street. Many older residents know it as the Milton Arms, as it used to a public house, a restaurant and a gift shop by the same name. Some years ago, the building was a restaurant, The Olive Grove, and more recently it houses a boutique and coffee shop.

The spirit haunting the building is rarely troublesome, but it does have a liking for pretty things, and will often cause the small carousel display of necklaces on the counter to rattle and sway. Occasionally, an item will go missing, but is later found back in its proper place. A worker there recalls experiencing a feeling of not being alone, but this did not perturb her, as she felt it was quite a nice sensation. The same worker is quite sure that she has felt a slight tap on her shoulder several times.

The Spice Ship

Originally named The Ship, the public bar is said to house the ghost of a Portuguese sailor who died around 200 years ago. Previous owners experienced a ship's bell, which hangs behind the bar, ringing of its own accord. Some family photos shot in the bar show the faint, shadowy image of an unknown man, standing either behind or to the side of those whose pictures are being taken. Alarms regularly being set off and ghostly footsteps in an empty building are other examples of the supernatural activity here. One former landlord even had the unpleasant experience of being pulled out of bed by an unseen presence. A present-day member of staff tells of glasses becoming so hot that they explode!

The ghost does seem to go for long periods of quiet, and activity generally reoccurrs either during or after refurbishment. One such period was when a small side-building was incorporated into the main bar area. This small building was allegedly used as a mortuary hundreds of years ago, and it is thought that this is where the Portuguese sailor's body was brought after he died aboard his ship.

The Colwell Centre

This is a small shopping centre housing a variety of independent traders. It was built in the mid-1980s on the site of Weymouth Royal Hospital (1871–1921), and during the First World War the hospital accommodated over 7,000 injured soldiers and sailors.

When the centre first opened, the downstairs sales floor had an arrangement of market-type stalls in the centre. A former trader from one of these stalls frequently found that stock on display had been rearranged during the night. She mentioned this to a trader in one of the lock-up units and they too had experienced the same thing; sometimes they arrived in the morning to find goods in their shop placed on the floor so that they formed a circle.

After a programme of refurbishment, the centre seemed to take on a sad and depressing atmosphere. Traders working late, after the centre closed for the day, periodically heard quiet sobs and moans, leading them to believe someone was locked in the building. Fire alarms would occasionally go off by themselves and during one of these alarms, smoke could be smelt strongly, but the attending fire officers could not find the source.

The centre has an unfortunate reputation for failed businesses, and some have said that the building is cursed because it stands on a place that saw so much misery and death.

Chesil Beach

Chesil Beach is a wide ridge of pebbles some eighteen miles long. It stretches from Portland to Abbotsbury, and the fishermen of old, coming ashore in the dead of night, could tell the exact point where they had landed by the size of the pebbles, which are around the size of a baby's head at the Portland end, gradually down to the size of pea shingle at Abbotsbury.

The Fleet Lagoon, which lies behind the beach, is a haven for wildlife and was the secret site for the testing of Barnes-Wallace's famous bouncing bomb. The shore-side of the beach offers unrivalled fishing and is a popular night-fishing venue for serious sea anglers.

There are countless reports of anglers hearing footsteps crunching along towards them in the dead of night. Thinking it is a fellow angler approaching, they are alarmed to discover they cannot see anyone in their torchlight. One poor angler caught more than a few mackerel one evening when, on hearing the footsteps, he was relieved to see a normal-looking old man, carrying equally old fishing gear, walking along the beach. The old man stopped to have a chat. Before moving on, the older man said that he usually fished the beach once a week for his supper.

About half an hour later, the angler noticed there was no sign of a light from where the old man went, so he thought he'd walk down and check on him. He walked for quite a distance and then came upon another angler. The second angler denied seeing or hearing anyone that evening, let alone an old man. Retracing his steps,

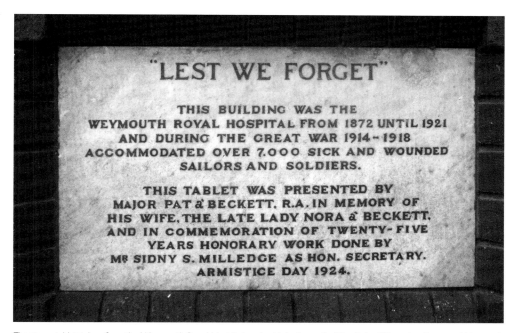

The stone tablet taken from the Weymouth Royal Hospital and set into the wall of the Colwell Shopping Centre, which stands on the site.

The magnificent sweep of Chesil Beach, a natural formation with many 'supernatural' happenings.

he realised that there was, indeed, no-one between his set up and the second angler. He had no idea where the old man could have gone. He had not heard any further footsteps, so the angler was sure the old man had not walked back past him, and as that part of the beach backed onto the Fleet, it was not possible for the old man to have left the beach by walking up and over the ridge. Vowing to never fish that part on his own again, the angler packed up his gear and left.

There are also reports of night fishermen hearing children laughing on the beach at West Bexington and further along at Abbotsbury. The laughs are described as those of young children rather than teens, and they always seem to be heard around 1 a.m.

Sadly, Chesil Beach has seen its share of tragic events. Several ships were lost offshore with much loss of life. On 25 November 1872, the *Royal Adelaide* was driven towards the most dangerous part of the beach at Portland, infamously christened 'Deadman's Bay'. The powerful undertow and pounding waves made rescue difficult, and some passengers and crew were swept away. Further deaths were caused by locals who 'salvaged' the barrels of alcohol when the ship's cargo was looted. At least four people literally drank themselves to death, or died from exposure, as they lay in a drunken stupor on the beach in midwinter.

Further tragedy happened on 11 September 1877, when in the middle of a force eight gale *The Forest* and *The Avalanche* collided off Portland Bill, with the loss of 115 lives. Several bodies were eventually washed ashore at Chiswell Cove. With such a history, is it any wonder that local legend abounds with tales of the men, women and children who perished that day, their moans and screams rising from the waves on stormy nights, their outlines moving in a line up the beach before disappearing into thin air?

Death found its way to Chesil Beach, not only from the sea but also from the air. The Fleet Lagoon, lying behind the bank, was used as a bombing range before and during the Second World War. Several fatal crashes, either directly into the beach or into the nearby waters, are recorded to have happened in the run up to the outbreak of hostilities, and dozens more afterwards, which resulted in the deaths of both allied and enemy airmen. One enduring story is that of a downed Luftwaffe officer, killed on impact, who still walks the beach on moonlit nights near to where his plane crashed. Could the footsteps heard by the Chesil anglers be those of the German pilot, or one of the many other souls claimed by the treacherous sea?

Balls of Light

A newspaper article from 2008 reported that a group of four walkers watched an unidentified flying object rising above Weymouth Bay. The group were standing outside the Prince Regent Hotel on the Esplanade at around 9.45 p.m., when they saw an unusual ball of orange light appear in the sky between Alexandra Gardens and the bay.

At first, they thought it was a firework, and then they realised it was travelling too slowly. The object rose higher and sported a straggling tail like a jellyfish. They watched as it veered left towards Bowleaze and disappeared into the outline of a triangle.

This is not the first report of strange orange-coloured lights. On winter nights, some say specifically on St Andrews day, one of the ancient earthworks known as 'barrows' (and known locally as Bincombe Bumps), situated near Bincombe on

Deadman's Bay, Portland. This beautiful cove belies a coast that claimed many lives and has been the scene of numerous shipwrecks. The screams and cries of victims are said to be heard on stormy nights.

Ridgeway Hill, is said to pour forth a column of flame that shoots upward with an orange intensity that tears open the night sky. The fiery pillar burns brightly for a few seconds, and then vanishes as abruptly as it appeared, leaving behind no trace of scorching or ash on the turf.

The last reported incident was in 1984. A young woman was riding pillion on her boyfriend's motorbike, which was travelling along the top road of Came Down. They were both startled to see flames suddenly shooting upward and a bright orange glow emitting from one of the many barrows upon the Ridgeway. The young couple thought the area had some sinister air about it and didn't stop to find out what caused this unusual phenomenon.

Again in the mid-1980s, a MoD Policeman, serving at Portland Naval Base, witnessed white balls of light coming out of the water at sporadic intervals, some 200 yards from the 'hood' entrance to the harbour on the seaward side.

The policeman observed the lights through binoculars as they rose in the air and disappeared. The time was 2.30 a.m. and the display went on for around ten minutes. There were no vessels on the surface of the water, and when the man spoke to both the Lulworth and Portland coastguards, they too had no idea what they were.

Note: While researching material for another chapter, I discovered that on

Bincombe Bumps.

5 April 1941, a German Heinkel He111 bomber crashed into Ridgeway Hill, as did a Hurricane Fighter in October of the same year. Sadly, almost a year to the day later another Hurricane, shrouded in mist, flew straight into the Ridgeway. Are the flames that have been sighted in the area actually a playback of one of these unfortunate planes meeting its destruction?

The Pit of Doom

During the development of the new Weymouth relief road, a pit containing dozens of neatly stacked human skulls and a huge assortment of bones were uncovered by archaeologists excavating the area on the top of Ridgeway Hill, prior to the start of the road building.

It was a particularly grisly find. It was thought, at first, that the remains were of the Iron Age residents of Maiden Castle, who had fallen victim to the Roman army invaders during a battle, or possibly even of the Romans themselves. Local paranormal enthusiasts believed that if this was correct, then maybe it explained the sightings of Roman soldiers marching along the Ridgeway; perhaps their ghosts were continuing the journey back to camp that their earthly bodies were unable to complete.

Scientists from NERC Isotope Geosciences Laboratory, analysed food and drink isotopes from the teeth of ten of the skulls, which revealed that the remains were very probably Scandinavian in origin, dating from AD 910 to 1030. The dismembered bodies of fifty-one men originally lay in what was found to be a disused Roman quarry, which was seemingly used by the killers for convenience instead of digging a fresh pit.

Archaeologists ascertained that the men were all killed at the same time, with large, sharp weapons such as swords. Many had failed to be dispatched cleanly and bore signs of having suffered multiple blows to the vertebrae, jawbones and skulls. One man had his hands sliced through, suggesting that he had attempted to grab the sword when it was swung towards him. They had no obvious battle wounds and so were most likely to have been captives. Judging from the lack of any remains of clothing or other possessions, they had probably been naked when they were thrown into the pit. There are more bodies than skulls, indicating that a couple of the heads, perhaps of high-ranking individuals, were kept as souvenirs or put on stakes.

Several theories have been put forward as to how these men ended up being killed so far away from home, but the one that seems to have the most credence is that during the period identified in the radiocarbon data tests, the native Saxons were at war with invading Vikings, and the unfortunate fifty-one were probably captured during a pillaging excursion and publicly executed.

All the remains have now been removed and the 'Pit of Doom', as it was christened, once more lies buried under the soil. Every day, hundreds of vehicles, thousands even in the summer season, will pass directly over what was the last resting place of over four dozen young men. It was quite an eerie coincidence that at the time of the discovery, a huge thunderstorm suddenly erupted over the site.

The Wyke Witch

At Wyke Regis (now a suburb of Weymouth), there once lived an old woman who was suspected of practising witchcraft. At that time, it was believed she had put a spell on a young local girl. A gypsy informed the girl's mother to hang a bullock's heart, stuffed with pins, inside the chimney, which in time would break the spell.

The mother followed these instructions, and when the heart dried out it fell into the fire and was burnt to a cinder. Later, when her daughter recovered, the spirit of the old witch was seen in a fit of rage, claiming that someone had been meddling in her affairs.

The block at Portland Castle. The ultimate Tudor punishment!

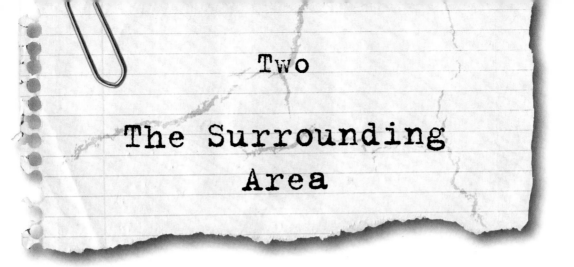

Two

The Surrounding Area

Portland Castle

Built by Henry VIII in the early 1540s to protect the large natural harbour from French and Spanish invasion, Portland Castle remains one of the best surviving examples of coastal defence from that period. There remains also several of its former occupants!

During the Civil War, the castle became a stronghold for the island's Royalists and was constantly under siege. Many bloody exchanges took place, and the garrison doctor, Richard Wiseman, often had to perform emergency surgery down in the castle's stone kitchen, where water and a huge fire were easily accessible. The fire was necessary because, in order to stop limbs becoming gangrenous, he would cauterise the men's wounds with a red-hot poker.

One can only imagine the screams of the men he attended; however, you may not have had to imagine the smell, as many people have been greeted by the nauseating stench of burning flesh when entering the kitchen.

In the early 1990s, head custodian Antoinette Woolvern entered Portland Castle in the middle of a raging thunderstorm. As she walked into the kitchen, she attempted to switch on the light, but all the bulbs blew. She was then overwhelmed with the odour of rotting flesh and a feeling of such incredible sadness that she wanted to break down and cry.

On another occasion, a six-year-old boy who had been happily enjoying exploring the castle, refused to go inside the kitchen and screamed the place down when his parents tried to encourage him down the steps.

The kitchen seems to be the centre of other unexplainable phenomenon. Because of its history, Portland Castle is often used by members of re-enactment societies. One such society, which had used the kitchen fireplace as part of their activities, went to bed leaving the hearth full of soot and embers, as they intended to clean it up in the morning when the remains had cooled. They came down early the next day to find the fireplace swept completely clean.

On another occasion, a woman from a different society took some photographs of her colleagues in the kitchen. When she developed the film, one of the prints had a swirling mist on it which wasn't on any of the other frames taken at the time.

The kitchen is also used as a wedding venue for small civil ceremonies. One guest

Portland Castle, a stronghold built by Henry VIII
to guard Portland Harbour.

The kitchen at Portland Castle, where the smell of rotting flesh
reminds visitors of the gory operations once carried out in this room.

at a wedding in 2008, who arrived a little early, decided to take her place inside as the day was hot. As the guest entered the kitchen doorway, she was aware of a female figure in a long dress, bustling about on the other side of the room. Thinking it was one of the castle's staff preparing the room for the wedding, she asked if it was alright to come in and sit down. The guest then watched as the figure turned and faded into thin air.

The Great Hall on the upper level, which still has its original Tudor floor, is another room in the castle that is used for weddings and re-enactment events.

One evening the Portland Garrison Civil War society held a banquet. The members of this garrison always stay faithful to the dances and tunes of the seventeenth century, and for one member it was an evening he would not forget. On his way back from the lavatory, he was merrily humming a tune of the period to himself when suddenly, he became aware of being accompanied by a spectral voice. He immediately stopped, but his unseen companion continued humming.

Castle staff, when working below or outside the Great Hall, regularly hear noises coming from that area, which they describe as sounds similar to those that would naturally happen if a family were living in there: various footsteps walking across the room, faint conversations and, sometimes, the rustle or sweep of a dress across the floor. New members of staff, when patrolling the building before locking up for the night, race upstairs upon hearing the footsteps and muted voices, believing some visitors are still present. They are always very surprised to discover the hall and adjoining rooms completely empty. Canine visitors,

The Great Hall at Portland Castle.

The 'Lavender Lady' staircase.

while seemingly happy in other areas, have refused to walk through the Great Hall.

The smell of lavender has often been reported to linger on a stone staircase leading to the upper floor. Staff believe the scent could belong to a woman they have christened 'The Lavender Lady', linked to Charles Manning – the last governor of Portland who lived there in the 1800s. Apparently, she hated living in the castle, and following a slow deterioration in her physical and mental health, she died within its walls. Children also resided in this home, and it would appear that some dwell here still. One young visitor, when asked by a member of the castle staff conducting a tour what he had enjoyed most, replied, 'I liked playing hide and seek with the little girl.' Nothing very strange about that, until the staff member realised there had been no other children on the tour.

One or more of the spirits seem to enjoy playing with the castle alarms, which are set off regularly all by themselves. After one incident involving the fire alarms, the curator called the fire brigade to attend and check it was, indeed, yet another false alarm. After ascertaining that all was well, a fireman and the curator were talking in a small room off the Great Hall, when she became aware of someone tugging at her clothes as if to gain her attention. Antoinette stepped forward, thinking her jacket may have been caught up on a piece of furniture but, on turning around to look, nothing was caught and, intriguingly, no-one was there.

Exactly the same experience was reported by another staff member in the vicinity – an area which is now known to have once housed a cannon.

Perhaps it's the same child who haunts another room on the first floor, seen by a custodian. After finishing her shift for the day, she casually looked up from the gun platform to an upstairs window, and was surprised to see a child aged about seven, with blonde hair, staring down at her. Thinking there were visitors still in the building, the custodian went up to investigate, only to find the rooms empty.

Baffled, she thought she'd solve the mystery by calling her son to come to the castle. She got him to stand at the window and try to leave the castle, unseen, before she reached the room from the gun platform below. It proved an impossible task.

Another youngster confided to his mother, while looking around the castle, that he didn't mind the ghosts, but he didn't like it when they ran right through him. Different members of staff have felt something 'walk through them', as well as experiencing extreme cold spots and becoming overwhelmed with emotion. There was even a time when one custodian unlocked the castle at the start of the day and refused to enter until company arrived!

One visitor felt an unseen presence push her while out on the castle ramparts, and a young boy, who is a regular visitor, claims to have had conversations with several ghosts in the rampart area.

Paranormal activity does not seem to be restricted to the castle alone. Within the courtyard stands an elegant two-storey building called the Captain's House. Once a brew house and stables, it was more recently used as officers' quarters. There have been reports that the upstairs taps turn on at will, a phenomenon which continues to this day. One day, a journalist researching the castle popped in to use the toilets. She left her inactive tape machine on a shelf in the cloakroom, but was astonished to hear it switch on and start to play all by itself.

The Heights Hotel

Visitors staying in this modern hotel are often surprised to see the figure of a Victorian lady, strolling though a corridor and disappearing into a bedroom without opening the door. While the hotel was built long after the era that the ghostly walker seems to belong to, it is constructed on land that was once, in times gone by, a very popular spot for promenading and 'taking the air'. Some would then travel the short distance to The Grove, where for sixpence they could take a seat at an upper-floor window in one of the houses along the road, to watch real-life convicts working in the nearby admiralty quarries. Maybe this phantom lady is eternally walking the path she took in the past, looking at the spectacular views which have remained unchanged over the years.

Pennsylvania Castle – Portland

The Penn Castle, as it is known locally, was built in 1800 for John Penn, military governor of the island and grandson of William Penn, the founder of the US state of Pennsylvania. Penn spent £20,000 (a huge sum in those days) to create his 'castle' on land, given to him by his friend King George III.

Set upon a hillside overlooking the stunningly beautiful Church Ope Cove, it comes as no surprise that in the 1980s, the building was converted into a hotel, and it was during the latter part of this decade that I worked there for a year as a waitress.

It was not long before employees here told of a 'presence' in the kitchen and in a small preparation area called the 'Still Room'. A senior waitress remembers being visited at work in the Still Room by her daughter and small grandchild. As the two women talked, they noticed the child seemingly playing peep-boo with an unseen person who, judging from the child's line of vision, was standing in a tiny passageway that lay between the Still Room and the Blue Room (an unused dining room which was once the castle's original kitchen area).

When questioned who she was playing with, the child replied, 'The lady in the white hat.' The feeling among the staff was that the ghost was a maidservant from the days of John Penn; this they guessed from the child's description of a white hat.

Even before being told the story, I had often felt that I was not alone in the Still Room and that someone was watching from the doorway leading to the Blue Room. This feeling was, at times, so intense that I would quickly turn from whatever task I was engaged in, hoping to catch a glimpse of whoever had been standing there.

Pennsylvania Castle.

There was a tiny storeroom off the passageway, which held brooms, mops and a couple of stools, where staff could have a crafty cigarette or sit down during service. On numerous occasions, while enjoying a quick break in this hideaway, I felt a cold draft whisk through the passageway, just as if someone had walked by. As both the Still Room and Blue Room did not have any doors leading directly to the outside, it was not possible for this chilly experience to have been the result of an open door.

The intense cold was also very noticeable in the Blue Room, and I avoided going in there if possible. However, as this room held the cutlery and crockery store cupboards, it was not somewhere that I could stay away from in the course of my duties. One particular week, in the summer of 1989,

the hotel played host to a group of healers and yoga practitioners who had hired the entire premises to hold a residential healing and retreat week. The Blue Room was given over to hosting the yoga classes, but at the end of the week one of the practitioners said that, even though the hotel was in such a wonderfully scenic location and her bedroom comfortable, she was glad to be leaving later that day. She had almost called a halt to her sessions several times, due to a feeling of hostility permeating the room, and because of the cold that, at times, felt as icy as deep winter.

Leading off the hotel kitchen was, at one time, the tradesmen's entrance and servants' area, with a narrow wooden staircase leading to an equally narrow upper corridor, from off which lay several small low ceiling bedrooms. Although at the time the rooms

Remains of the entrance to St Andrew's Church.

A pirate's tomb?

The atmospheric ruins of St Andrew's Church, clinging to the east side of the island.

were part of the hotel, from their size and position it would be safe to assume they were formerly the servants' quarters. At times, I had to go up to these rooms to collect service trays, and that same feeling of not being alone was present here too. One time, I even felt someone pass me by as I bent down to pick up a tray. I thought it might have been a guest trying to get past, so I apologised, but when I stood up I realised that there was in fact nobody there.

Pirates Graveyard – Portland

Between the Penn Castle, on the hillside, and the rocks of Church Ope Cove below, stand the ruins of St Andrew's Church.

There's a small woodland footpath to the ruins, which leads down from the northern edge of the castle grounds.

Built in the thirteenth century, St Andrews served as the parish church for the island, but was abandoned in the eighteenth century due to continued landslips, and some say raids, by French pirates. It is the pirate legacy that has led to a gravestone, carved with the infamous skull and crossbones, being hailed in tourist guidebooks as the pirate's grave. People do, indeed, make the trip down the precarious path to view it.

It is probably not really a pirate's grave, as the graves of plague victims sometimes bore this symbol, or it was just used to symbolise death itself. What is certain though, is the sound of soft chanting heard on summer evenings. Former hotel guests relaxing with their bedroom windows open have heard it, as have walkers in the area. The ruins have a reputation of being a centre for the practice of black magic or pagan rituals, so whether the chanting is supernatural in origin, or from a human source, is open to debate. One walker, who claims to have heard the

Is this another pirate's resting place, or just the stonemason using the traditional symbol of death to adorn the gravestone?

Church Ope Cove,
where a mermaid reputedly came ashore.

sounds, apparently climbed up to the ruins and found the place deserted.

Interestingly, a mermaid is reputed to have actually once come ashore at Church Ope Cove. It was spotted as the people were going to a service at St Andrew's Church. Some versions of the tale suggest she was taken up to the church, where she died the next day.

Devil Dogs

Throughout the land, there are various reports of large spectral black dogs, commonly known as 'shucks'. Portland boasts at least one, if not three, of these creatures.

The Roy Dog is believed to have his lair either in or near a formation known as Cave Hole, which is situated close to the lighthouse at Portland Bill. This animal is described as a shaggy black dog, as tall as a man and sporting one green and one fiery red eye. A further horror is that the freshly plucked eyes of its victims can be seen entwined in his mane of dark fur.

Local legend recalls that two men from further up the Isle, along with the lighthouse keeper, were fishing near Portland Bill one evening after a hard day's work.

As dusk fell, the two men bid the keeper goodnight and prepared to make their way back to their respective homes. The keeper chose to spend a few more moments alone, to enjoy the peace of the early evening before climbing the steps to light the lamp.

The two men had not gone far from their fishing spot when their surroundings slowly faded into half-darkness. One

Portland Bill, home to the fearsome Roy Dog.

of them heard a sound from behind and, as he peered into the gloom, he spotted what seemed to be lights moving towards them. As the lights came closer, he saw that one light glowed red and the other glowed an unearthly green. The man shuddered; he'd heard talk of a monstrous creature with glowing eyes but never imagined that he would witness it. Realising the thing was nearly upon them, he ducked behind a large bush, dragging his friend with him. The men held their breath and watched as a dark mass of fur stumbled past the bush. They noticed that the creature seemed to hobble as though in pain. To their horror, the creature stopped to drink from a pool of water and to lick a ragged paw, before limping off into the night. Once the creature had gone, the men noticed that there was no light shining from the lighthouse. Fearing the worst, they ran back to their fishing spot, and among the rocks they found the body of the lighthouse keeper, his face frozen in a mask of terror; he had literally been scared to death. When the keeper's line was pulled from the water, a lump of flesh and the claw of a huge hound were dangling on the end.

The Tow Dog, while still frightening to encounter, is a much less horrifying sight. The creature, once again, resembles a very large black dog with luminous red eyes, but instead of attacking or causing harm to the humans encountered, it merely stands its ground and blocks their path. Some claim that the Tow Dog is an omen of ill fortune or death; others view it as more of a warning.

Although the Roy Dog is reputed to inhabit the south of the Island, and the Tow Dog appears mostly on the west side, there are a few other reports about a similar creature that stalks the East Weares, but who seems more timid and has only been spotted from a distance. One local lady, walking her dog along the Weares, thought she saw what appeared to be a large, unaccompanied dog a little way ahead, standing near to the path she was taking. Knowing her own dog, a spaniel called Archer, sometimes had issues with other dogs, she called him to heel and put on his lead. When she looked up at the path again, the other dog had gone. Just in case it reappeared, she kept the lead on Archer and continued up the path. All was well until she reached the spot where she had first seen the black dog. At this point, Archer began to behave strangely and refused to walk any further. He acted in a distressed manner, whining and pulling on the lead in an attempt to get away from the area. As it was getting close to dusk, the woman led Archer back down the path and onto the old railway-line bank. Archer regained his usual composure and his owner thought no more about it, until she looked back towards the small path where the incident had happened and, once again, for a few fleeting moments she saw the unmistakable form of a large black dog, standing to one side of the path.

Time Slip

Portland and Weymouth were major embarkation ports for troops involved in the D-Day landings of the Second World War.

While walking his dog early one quiet May morning in 1976, Mr Murphy suddenly found himself surrounded by tanks, jeeps and American soldiers walking around. Then, as suddenly as they had appeared, the scene vanished, leaving both Murphy and his dog shaking. The witness speculated that he had witnessed a brief moment when soldiers were making final preparations for the D-Day landings.

High Angle Batteries on Portland.

Inside the ammunition bunkers.

The High Angle Battery

Known to all Portland children as the ghost tunnels, the site dates from Victorian times and served as part of Britain's coastal defenses. The 'high angle' refers to the operation of the huge 12-ton guns, which fired shells upwards at a height that ensured they dropped down to inflict maximum damage on the less sheilded upper decks of any attacking vessel, the sides of which were usually clad in iron.

Built into a quarry pit so as to be hidden from enemy view, the gun emplacements were fed with ammunition via a railway from underground magazines. Also underground were duty accommodation and shelters for the men who served here.

Although dangerous, it's almost a rite of passage for the area's youngsters to walk through the dark tunnels that are no longer gated, and this is usually executed with much pushing, nervous giggling and egging on by their friends. One fine Sunday afternoon in the early spring of 1990, a group of young people from the nearby Grove-area of Portland, were playing close to the battery when one of the party spotted someone standing at the end of one of the tunnels. He proposed it would be a good laugh for the group to quietly enter the other end and make ghostly noises.

They all agreed, and once they were in place at the edge of the tunnel, they could hear the sound of talking coming from the other end. They proceeded with the plan and started their eerie groans, fully expecting whoever was at the other end to register a loud vocal surprise. There was no response and, realising this, they stopped and looked at one another in puzzlement. One of them ran round to the other end and found no-one. When she arrived back, the rest of the group reported that no-one had emerged out of the tunnel either. They assumed the people they had heard had simply walked off elsewhere on the site.

As the group prepared to leave, they noticed that everything had suddenly gone very quiet; no birds sang and neither could they hear the breeze or the buzzing of insects. Then came an intense feeling of being watched; one of the group members later described it as though he was a rat in a lab experiment and someone was watching over his every move. The spell was broken when stones were thrown at the group; but it was not possible to see who was doing the throwing, nor from which direction the stones were coming from. They had had enough, and each ran screaming up the bank. One young man did give a backwards glance though. He was shocked to see the figure of a man, seemingly laughing at their fleeing forms. The young man alerted one of his friends, who turned round to see only thin air where the laughing man had stood. Did a ghostly soldier turn the tables on a bunch of trick-playing young people,

or was it a real person having a little fun himself? The group didn't wait to find out!

Many others have reported similar experiences in the vicinity of the tunnels, myself included. A particular incident that I cannot explain was when I decided to explore one of the side rooms that lie off each side of the main tunnel. As the tunnel has a bend in the middle, no natural light filters through, leaving the side rooms pitch black. Knowing this, I had taken a torch and switched it on as I entered the tunnel. I made my way into one of the side rooms, as planned, but was somewhat perturbed when the torchlight began to flicker and fade. I knew the batteries to be almost new, and as I looked down at the torch, I felt the unmistakable touch of a hand on my shoulder and then a brush down my upper arm. The torchlight then came back to full strength and I concluded that I had had enough of playing explorer for that day!

One of the tunnel entrance gates.

Several years later, a husband and wife holidaying on the Island came upon the battery during an afternoon walk. They decided to have a look around the site and the tunnels, but it was a decision one of them was to later regret. After a peaceful thirty minutes or so wandering around the buildings and gun emplacements, the couple made their way into a tunnel. However, their progress was no more than a few steps when the husband felt a searing pain on the top of his head and fell down. Blood was pouring from the wound, much to the distress of his wife. Even more alarming was that there did not seem any logical reason for the cause of the injury. Fortunately, it was only a flesh wound and the man made a full recovery.

Note: This report is very similar to an incident I witnessed myself while showing two visiting ghost hunters around the site, again in the afternoon. On entering a tunnel, one of the men clasped his head in pain and he was found to have sustained a head wound. It was thought at the time that he had perhaps banged his head on the crosspiece of an overhead metal grating, but it did seem strange that many people, including myself, had entered this tunnel without harm on several occasions, and the metal grating was still attached in to the roof of the tunnel at exactly the same height.

Abbotsbury

This small village is best known for its superb, subtropical gardens and its Swannery, but if you scratch a little beneath the surface, you find an underbelly of murder and illegal activity.

One of the most spooky areas at night is a small lane known as New Barn Road.

A little way past the entrance to the Swannery, the road climbs and then drops steeply. It's quite a dark roadway, on account of there being no street-lighting for miles around. It's common to encounter patches of swirling mist late at night, which only serves to heighten the ghostly atmosphere. This generally doesn't bother locals, who are used to using New Barn Road as an alternative route from the hamlets of Rodden and Elworth to Abbotsbury, but one night, a married couple on holiday were trying to find their way back to their accommodation at Burton Bradstock, after enjoying a meal in Langton Herring. They took a wrong turn and found themselves not on the main B3157 road, but driving along a narrow lane. They decided to carry on along the lane, joking that it would be a little adventure. What they did not realise at the time was just how true those words were going to be.

Some way before the Swannery car park, there is a small copse at the bottom of a hill. As the couple were travelling along, they saw something in their headlights run across the road into the trees. Presuming it was a deer, they slowed down in case it decided to run back out in front of their car. Suddenly, the engine seemed to be drained of power and the car slowed to a halt. The husband got out of the car to see what was wrong and, despite it being a warm summer night, he felt icy cold and a little uneasy. Before he could lift the bonnet, his wife became alarmed by a light moving around in the copse. The man saw a faint glow darting in and out and shouted to ask who was there. Suddenly, the car sprung back into life and the icy chill faded. As they drove off, the husband looked in his rear-view mirror and was sure that he saw a glowing shape travel out from the copse into the field across the road.

There are reports of residents encountering a glowing man in a wide-brimmed

New Barn Road. A holidaying couple got a little more adventure than they had bargained for during a night-time drive along this road.

hat, dressed in seventeenth-century clothing, near the same spot. History records that in Abbotsbury at the time of the Civil War, Royalists were constantly being hunted by Cromwell's men. The wide-brimmed hat worn by the glowing phantom does seem to fit the description of those typically worn by King Charles' supporters.

The Ilchester Arms Hotel

Once a coaching inn on the London to Exeter route, it is now a warm and welcoming public bar and hotel which, along with serving fine ales and food, boasts an interesting assortment of ghosts!

A ghostly Charles stands near to the great fireplace and is in the habit of jangling coins in his hands. He was the gatekeeper and stable master in the inn's heyday. The coins are the ones given to him in payment for the stabling and care of the coach horses.

According to a visiting psychic medium, Charles is the head of the spirit family that inhabits the building. He also takes it upon himself to watch over the bar and, apparently, will not allow anyone he dislikes to sit in the vicinity of, what he seems to consider, his domain by the fireplace. One of the present owners confirms this, saying that she has watched someone make for the seats in that area, and then when they arrive there, for no reason they suddenly seem to change their mind and make for a table in a different part of the bar. Although few people have seen Charles, a number have heard the jingling of coins when no earthly person can be seen to be responsible for the noise.

It's claimed that on the upper floors there is the spirit of one child, or possibly two children, who delight in tripping up one of the residents. This resident also reports that she often feels like she is about to walk into a wall, even though there is no wall to be

The Ilchester Arms fireplace, where Charles stands in watch.

The Ilchester Arms. The site of the original entrance for coaches is still visible and, behind the window to the right of the picture, is the present-day ladies' toilet area, where the phantom woman is seen.

seen. The medium who identified Charles also confirmed that one child, in particular, is quite attached to the resident, and her frequent trips and feelings of there being a wall are simply this child's way of being playful with her; there is no intention to cause harm. The resident does not mind this and takes the opportunity everyday to greet the child, or children.

One of the more startling apparitions is that of an upper part of a Victorian lady, who, aptly enough, is seen in the ladies' toilets. Investigations by the owners have discovered that the ladies' toilets were built on an area that was once outside, and where people stood while waiting to board the coach. Furthermore, the level of the floor in the modern-day toilets is much higher than the ground in the coaching inn days, so it would seem the lady is still standing on the original level.

A number of people have seen a phantom dog walk through the bar and also in the conservatory; it is described as quite friendly and very hairy. Some years ago a photo was taken in the conservatory, which showed a faint image of a dog when there were no dogs present.

On one occasion, the chef was in the bar talking to a man and woman who were having a quiet drink. The chef was standing with his back to the bar and, after a while, he noticed that the woman kept looking over his shoulder as he talked. The chef turned round, only to find that there was nothing. Intrigued, he politely asked what she was looking at. The woman professed to have psychic vision and casually stated that the bar was busy that night with a crowd of American GIs. She went on to add that they were from the north of England and on holiday in Dorset, but she had no knowledge about the hotel's haunted reputation; they had merely thought it a nice

place to stop for a drink and bite to eat, on a day out exploring the Jurassic coast route.

Although the chef knew about the hotel's various ghosts, he had never heard mention about GIs, so was a little sceptical about the authenticity of the supposed sighting. Some months later, however, during a totally unconnected conversation, an elderly resident happened to mention that the US army conducted exercises in the area prior to D-Day, and often GIs would come over to Abbotsbury from their camps along Chesil Beach, and the bar at the Illchester Arms was a popular place for them to have a drink and a spot of fun.

Quite the opposite of fun is the ghost of a man that haunts the kitchen. He is described as a menacing presence, and those who encounter him feel as though he would have been quite a nasty fellow in life. The first time one of the owners set eyes on him was late one night, after the evening food service had finished. She was attending to the coffee machine when she glimpsed a man coming into the kitchen. Not turning to fully look at him, she politely told the man that the kitchen was closed and carried on with cleaning the machine. Aware that he was still standing, she repeated that the kitchen had closed and, this time, she turned round fully. Standing in the doorway was the terrible figure of a man dressed in a long black cloak and hood. She described the part of his face that could be seen as horrible and evil.

The same man has been seen by female relatives of the owners, one of whom ran screaming from the kitchen and now refuses to go in there.

A more benign spirit residing in the kitchen is that of a monk, who likes to make his presence felt by tugging at the chef's clothing and moving kitchen implements. As the name of the village suggests, there was indeed a Benedictine monastery nearby, which was ruined during King Henry VIII's Dissolution of the Monasteries. So, if the ghostly monk is a remnant from that age, it is likely that he predates the other spirits involved in the haunting, as the abbey at Abbotsbury was dissolved in 1538.

Baglake House – Litton Cheney

On 17 January 1748, in Long Bredy near Abbotsbury, a burial was recorded of William Light of Baglake Farm, Litton Cheney. The stories surrounding his death were recounted by a Miss M.F. Billington, in her article featured in the *Dorset County Chronicle*, in August 1883:

Bagley House, near Bridport, has very gloomy legends attaching to it. Tradition (for the stories are traced back to the last century) says that Squire Lighte, who then owned the place, had been hunting one day, and after returning home had gone away again and drowned himself. His groom had followed him with a presentiment that something was wrong, and arrived at the pond in time to see the end of the tragedy. As he returned he was accosted by the spirit of his drowned master, which unhorsed him. He soon fell violently ill, and never recovered. One of the consequences of this illness being that his skin peeled entirely off.

Shortly after Squire Lighte's suicide, his old house was troubled by noisy disturbances, which were at once associated with the evil deed of self-destruction. It was suggested that the spirit should be formally and duly 'laid', or exorcised. A number of the clergy went, therefore, for this very purpose, and succeeded in inducing the ghost to confine itself to a chimney in the house for a certain number of years. Miss Billington added:

For many years the place remained at peace but on the expiration of the power of the charm very much worse disturbances broke out again. Raps would be heard at the front door; steps in the passage and on the stairs; doors would open and close. The rustle of ladies dressed in silk was audible in the drawing-room, and from that room the sound was traced into a summer-house in the garden. The crockery would all be violently moved, and at certain rare intervals a male figure, dressed in old-fashioned costume, is said to have made itself visible and walked about the house. The neighbours say that these extraordinary occurrences continued for many years. They believe in them most fervently; and are of opinion that as long as the house stands it will be thus troubled. An element worthy of notice in this story is the time-honoured faith in the power of the clergy over evil spirits.

Lulworth – Flowers Barrow

Overlooking Lulworth Cove stand the Purbeck Hills, and high above the sea stands Flowers Barrow, a hill fort that was taken over by the Romans.

It is said that when conditions are right, a Roman army appears marching over the hills. Some say that they reappear in times of great unrest, with the last sighting occurring during the Second World War. Others claim that their arrival presages danger.

Some of the sightings have involved the sound of horses and the clashing of arms, and one seventeenth-century sighting was of such a huge force that local authorities sent word to London to expect a rising by the Catholics.

Lulworth Castle

This fine building was built in the reign of King James I, not as a defensive structure but as a hunting lodge for the King's visits.

In the early seventeenth century, the castle was bought by the Weld family, whose descendants still own the castle and surrounding land today. The castle was badly damaged by fire in 1929, and the three upper floors were totally destroyed. Nowadays, visitors can explore the restored shell of the castle's ground floor and servant areas, and a staircase goes up to the top of one of the towers, giving wonderful views all around the castle.

One afternoon, a visiting family of four adults and four children ascended the staircase, followed by another couple and their child. After reaching the top and spending ten minutes or so looking at the views, they decided to make their way back to the main hall. About half-way down the metal stair case, all the adults felt an overwhelming feeling of deep depression come over them, and the children commented on feeling 'funny'. The adults also experienced a bad ache in their right legs. As they reached the bottom of the stairs, the depressed feeling lifted as quickly as it had come. When asked, the other couple and child also reported feeling sad and having an ache in the legs at a similar spot on the staircase.

A member of the castle staff confirms that oppressive feelings on the first-floor

Lulworth Cove.

landing and staircase are very common, along with the sound of people walking up and down the last set of steps, when they know there is no-one there due to the place being closed to the public.

One visitor had a very uncomfortable experience on the first-floor landing, as he was pushed to the ground by an unseen force. There are also regular reports of a young female child, in Victorian-style dress, playing hide and seek in the basement. She runs behind the beds on display there, and she is often spotted running up and down the steps to the basement.

Paranormal sightings are not a recent phenomenon here. Two hundred years ago, a room in the castle would be inexplicably illuminated by an eerie radiance at night. It was said that it glowed so brightly, and caused so much consternation, that the room was once knocked down and rebuilt, only for it to start radiating the mysterious light again.

Lulworth Cove

During the Second World War, Lulworth Cove, along with all other beaches and coves which might offer a suitable landing place to German invaders, was closed to the public. The beach was strewn with mines and barbed wire, while the road leading inland was blocked with anti-tank traps and other obstacles. It was, quite simply, impossible for anyone to get on or off the beach by land or sea. To make doubly certain that the area was protected against Hitler's invading hordes, lookouts were posted on the hills to sweep the seas and skies with binoculars.

It was with some amazement that, at night, the lookouts saw people down on the beach. They seemed to be dancing in the moonlight. Then, as suddenly as they had appeared, they were gone. The area was carefully searched, and the defences tested and repositioned. But a few weeks later, the dancers were back.

It subsequently emerged that the phantom dancers had been seen before. A yachtsman who anchored in the cove in the 1930s, reported that the young people had attracted his attention when they waded up out of the sea, and only later did they dance on the sands.

A sailor who was anchored at Durdle Door claimed to have heard a scream coming from the shore. Then he saw some young girls appear from the water and start to dance, before fading and disappearing from view.

There have been many theories as to the origin of the phantom dancers. Some say they are mermaids, celebrating their transformation into human girls for one night of the year; another explanation is that they are a group of female maidservants that supposedly fled Lulworth Castle when it was gutted by fire on Thursday, 29 August 1929. Apparently, they were last seen running and screaming in the direction of Durdle Door.

In addition to the dancers, Napoleon, or a figure looking very much like the military leader, is said to appear along this stretch of coastline accompanied by another man. Napoleon looks at maps, before folding them up and vanishing along with his unidentified sidekick.

Within Lulworth village, it is said that a glowing ball of light haunted a farmer for several days, and it was believed to be his wife. This particular haunting stopped after he gave away the wife's possessions. However, more recently, there are reports of a phantom old lady seen near to the house.

The old RAF Warmwell rifle range, uncovered during preparation of land for building in 2007.

Warmwell

RAF Warmwell was a Battle of Britain fighter-base, used by both British and USA air forces between 1937 and 1946, when it was abandoned.

Post 1946 saw a proportion of the base disappear under houses being built to form the new residential development of Crossways. Another section became part of a holiday camp, known then as North Heath Holiday Park. I stayed at this park as a young teenager during the early 1970s and one day, along with a couple of friends, decided to go exploring through the bushes and trees surrounding the park. We eventually stumbled upon a cluster of derelict buildings. As I'd been studying the Second World War at school, the buildings looked to be of a similar style to pictures I'd seen of RAF and army bases of that time.

A couple of the buildings seemed reasonably intact, and so we ventured in to have a closer look. Suddenly, we heard footsteps, and fearing that we would be discovered and accused of trespassing, we turned to quickly leave. We received the fright of our lives when a man in uniform passed by the window. We ducked down and hoped he would not see us, but it was then that we received another fright, as one of the chairs behind us fell over, seemingly of its own accord.

Not caring if we did get caught now, we ran out of that building and away from the area as quick as our legs would carry us. One in the group risked a backwards glance and swore he momentarily saw a man, in a light-blue uniform, standing in the doorway of the building we had been in.

On arriving back at the park we vowed not to tell anyone, especially our parents as we should not have been in the place. Needless to say none of us were ever brave enough to make a return visit to the buildings!

Many years later, after moving to Dorset, I was employed as Entertainment Host at Warmwell Holiday Park. The North Heath site I'd stayed on as a teenager was now a residential mobile-home park, and the new holiday centre had been built a little further down the road. Being in that area reminded me of the old buildings and my strange experience as a young holidaymaker, and I mentioned it in passing to one of the maintenance staff at Warmwell Park. This gentleman had lived in the area all of his life, and he confirmed that the buildings we'd explored were those of RAF Warmwell. He also said that the bottom end of the park had been built on what was a section of the old airfield.

He also told me about the ghost of an airman, said to haunt that part of the park. The story goes that the airman got into difficulty one foggy night and tried to land at RAF Warmwell. Unfortunately, he crashed his plane and was killed. A couple of years later, a young corporal on night-guard duty was resting in the guard hut on the airfield, when he heard a plane approaching. Again, it was a foggy night. The plane landed and the pilot emerged and walked over to the hut. The airman claimed he had lost his squadron in the bad weather and asked if he could rest at the station until daylight, upon which he would leave for his own base. The corporal recognised the airman's accent as American, or Canadian, and escorted him up to the base of the control tower.

On returning to the hut, he found the plane gone. Thinking that the airman had somehow returned to the plane and taken off without being seen, the corporal logged the incident and settled back to complete his watch.

The following day, the corporal could not get the events of the previous night off his mind, so paid a visit to the control tower. Here he discovered that there was no record of any airman coming to see them, or of any plane landing or taking off.

There were more encounters with the lost airman during the time RAF Warmwell was in operation, and he is now alleged to be seen, on occasions, wandering around the holiday park that stands on the former airfield. He has been sighted by visitors and park workers alike – usually the security personnel making their nightly rounds.

Bibliography

North, M.J. & Newland, R.J., *Dark Dorset Tales of Mystery, Wonder and Terror* (CFZ Press, 2007)

Pomeroy, C., *Wings Over Weymouth* (The Dovecote Press, 2005)

http://daveg4otu.tripod.com/dorset/dorcrash.html

www.darkdorset.co.uk

www.wikipedia.org

Other titles published by The History Press

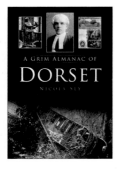

A Grim Almanac of Dorset

NICOLA SLY

A Grim Almanac of Dorset is a day-by-day catalogue of 365 ghastly tales from around the county. Full of dreadful deeds and a multitude of mysteries, it explores the darker side of Dorset's past. Here are stories of tragedy, torment and the truly unfortunate. Discover accounts of highwaymen, duellists, murderers, tragic suicides and bizarre deaths, includin the woman who tripped over a dog in Weymouth in 1878, and a soldier who dozed off while smoking on top of the Nothe Fort in 1877 and fell off the parapet.

978-0-7524-5884-7

Haunted Southampton

PENNY LEGG

Explore the darkest secrets of Southampton's past with this collection of startling stories. From the Roman soldiers who pervade Bitterne Manor to the Grey Lady at the Royal Victoria Country Park, the site of a former military hospital, the city is host to spirits no yet departed, who send a shiver down the spines of the living. Southampton is 'alive' wit ghosts and, for those who dare, the stories can be discovered in this chilling book.

978-0-7524-5519-8

Growing Up in Wartime Southampton: Someone Else's Trouser

JAMES MARSH

Spanning some of the most turbulent decades in recent world history, James Marsh reveals the gritty determination, community spirit and, above all, the humour with whic the local community faced the difficulties of war. Moving on to describe the harsh lessons learned in the 1940s and '50s schooling system, and subsequently describing his teenage years in the merchant navy, this book explores how growing up in the post-war years was both a challenge and a lot of fun.

978-0-7524-5840-3

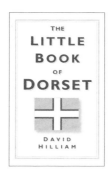

The Little Book of Dorset

DAVID HILLIAM

The Little Book of Dorset is a funny, fast-paced, fact-packed compendium of the sort of frivolous, fantastic or simply strange information which no-one will want to be without The county's most unusual crimes and punishments, eccentric inhabitants, famous sons and daughters, royal connections and literally hundreds of wacky facts about Dorset's landscape, fossil-rich coast, towns and villages (plus some authentically bizarre bits of historic trivia), come together to make it essential reading for visitors and locals alike.

978-07524-5704-8

Visit our website and discover thousands of other History Press books.

www.thehistorypress.co.uk